10 COSMIC DIMENSIONS

A Spiritual Guidebook to Ascension

Raven Shamballa

M.S. Counseling, Spiritual Teacher, Pranic Healer, Hypnotherapist

BALBOA.
PRESS

A DIVISION OF HAY HOUSE

Balboa Press books may be ordered through booksellers or by contacting:

Balboa Press
A Division of Hay House
1663 Liberty Drive
Bloomington, IN 47403
www.balboapress.com
1 (877) 407-4847

Raven Shamballa is the spiritual name of Monica Kelly.
Monica Kelly is Licensed Marriage and Family Therapist in the state of California #50615.

ISBN: 978-1-9822-0794-6 (sc)
ISBN: 978-1-9822-0795-3 (e)

Library of Congress Control Number: 2018908071

Print information available on the last page.

Balboa Press rev. date: 05/15/2019

Other Books by Raven Shamballa

**An Illustrated Guide
to the 7 Primary Chakras**

Receive a Free E-Book Download. This E-book presents an illustrated guide to the 7 Primary Chakras. These images are meant to be a learning tool for understanding the emotional and energetic poles of the chakras. Each of the 7 Primary Chakras have psychological themes and express both positive and negative emotions and energetic moods and behaviors.

In the table that accompanies the illustrations, I provide affirmations you can use with each chakra to open and balance the chakras. There is a quick reference listing the Attributes or Characteristics to the 7 chakras. There is a table where you can easily determine if a chakra is in balance or out of balance. This is a great learning tool to help you learn more about the 7 Primary Chakras.

**For a free download
of An Illustrated Guide
to the 7 Primary Chakras,
please visit www.ravenlightbody.com**

**The 100 Chakra Book, An Introduction
to Negative Energy Release Work**

This is the foundation teaching material for Raven energy healing practice Negative Energy Release Work (NERW). Raven introduces the concept that humans have 100 chakras, and advanced souls have up to 500 chakras. In the 100 Chakra book, Raven gives a detailed explanation of the 7 Primary Charkas, The Higher Chakras and the Ascending Chakras. She discusses the similarities and differences in the energy body and the soul body, and dives into exoteric concepts of the Higherself, and consciousness. She touches on developing your psychic abilities and working with your angelic team.

NERW has an emphasis on removing negative energies from the energy body, while expanding the soul body in meditation. A self-study, self-healing course is offered in the book to familiarize you with the concepts of the work.

**To receive a free energy healing
self-study course
on the 100 Chakra System,
please visit www.ravenlightbody.com**

The 3 Pendulum Languages

In this book, Raven explains how you can use the Pendulum to start communicating with your white light angelic team. Raven teaches how to contact your angelic team and start communicating with them. Raven's pendulum on the hand language gives a detail explanations of how you can advance your pendulum practice from simple Yes/No/Maybe questions to developing conversations with your team. Raven also explains techniques for working with charts and maps to receive more information.

The 3 Pendulum Languages contains 15 pendulum charts to assist you in conceptualizing a new way to receive information from your angels. Blank charts are provided for you to start your own journey into using this divination tool. Using the pendulum as a tool for angel communication is discusses as a training tool to help develop clairaudience, the ability to hear messages from your angels.

**To receive a free download
of the Angel Pendulum Chart,
go to www.ravenlightbody.com**

The 10 Cosmic Dimensions, A Spiritual Guidebook to Ascension

In the book, The 10 Cosmic Dimensions, A Spiritual Guidebook to Ascension, Raven shares information she has received from her guides and the Ascended Masters. She explains the concepts of karma, past lives, life between lives and the Light Realms. The cosmic dimensional scale is a measure of human spiritual evolution. Understanding where you are on the scale and in relationship to other people helps to give insight as to your spirit growth and how to interact with others, especially those lower on the cosmic dimensional scale.

This book includes a self-study course with 10 worksheets to assist you in understanding where you are on the scale.

**To receive a free chapter,
visit www.ravenlightbody.com**

Chakra Balancing with the Pendulum

In the book, Chakra Balancing with the Pendulum, Raven explores the language of the pendulum when working with the 7 Primary Chakras. This book teaches how to read your own chakras and how to balance them. It also gives information on how to read clients' chakras and assist them to balance. Certification courses in Negative Energy Release Work and Chakra Balancing will be taught in the future.

**For a free download,
go to www.ravenlightbody.com**

For more information on these topics stay connected!

YouTube:
Raven Shamballa

Facebook:
Raven Lightbody

Instagram:
ravenshamballalightbody

Pinterest:
ravenlightbody

About The Author

Monica Kelly grew up Clovis, CA. Her parents were immigrants. Her mom was born in Rio de Janeiro, Brazil and her father was born in Calcutta, India. After her father was converted at a Billy Graham crusade, he decided to become a Christian minister in America. Monica grew up within a strong Christian faith. During adolescence, there was a betrayal in the church which caused Monica to leave the church.

In college, Monica decided to practice hatha yoga to explore her Indian roots. That led to countless workshops on the subject and living at the Ananda Yoga Community in Seattle which introduced her to meditation, Kriya yoga and Raja Yoga. She returned to Fresno for graduate school. She graduated as a Marriage and Family Therapist at California State University, Fresno, in 2008. After graduation she discovered energy work, spiritual hypnosis and past life regression.

In 2014, she awoke from an operation as a full-blown psychic healer. Monica was told she had a near death experience, went to the Light Realms and it was decided by her Counsel of Masters to wake her up so she could develop a new system of energy healing called Negative Energy Release Work. She was also told she would bring forward information on the 100 Chakras.

At the conclusion of writing this book, Monica's Masters informed her it was time to change her name to Raven Shamballa. Her spiritual mission was made known to her.

Raven lives in Carlsbad, CA, where she works as an energy healer, psychic and psychotherapist. She continues to write books, lead meditations and expand the content of this work online. For more information, see her website www.ravenlightbody.com, search 'Raven Shamballa' on YouTube, search 'Raven Lightbody' on Facebook, search 'ravenshamballalightbody' on Instagram.

Readings are available by phone, Skype or in person in Oceanside, CA. Psychic readings are given on past lives, finding your life purpose, angel names, relationship issues, advancing in spiritual practice, psychic development and galactic origins. Negative Energy Release Work is an energy healing technique taught by Raven in which negative energies foreign to the energy body and Lightbody are released. For more information on this, see her website.

Acknowledgements

Thank you to my former husband John Kelly for all his love and support during the process of writing this book. I appreciate his encouraging words to follow my path, take charge of my career, and to be independent and strong. His support allowed me time to meditate, spiritually seek and grow in my wisdom. We had a beautiful relationship.

I want to thank my mom, Sonia Patnaik. She has been there over the years watching me grow and evolve on my path. Although my work in spiritual hypnosis has challenged her, she too listened to my stories. She was there when I went through my operation and psychic awakening. She has witnessed my growth in the light and has been there for me.

I thank all my yoga instructors. I am in gratitude to the Seattle Ananda Community, for all I learned during my stay there in the yoga community. I want to thank Dr. Garcia at California State University of Fresno for his support during my time in studying to be a Marriage and Family Therapist. He gave me the freedom to be a spiritualist within the framework of western psychology.

Thank you to all the support staff that had a hand in putting this book together. To my son, Darshan Davis.

Thank you again, Divine Source and the Ascended Masters. I am profoundly humbled and grateful for this mission. May we wake up as many people as possible. May Lightworkers everywhere learn to directly connect to Divine Source to ask their own questions and receive their own answers. Let us bring light to the world!

Divine Source and the White Light Masters that support and

guide me. Thank you for honoring me with your daily presence.

Thank you for teaching me directly this information that

I might share it with whomever is interested in learning sacred

knowledge. Thank you for being close to whomever seeks your

guidance and healing.

May we all learn to reach up and receive many blessings.

I am truly honored and blessed to behold the company

of Masters and it is my sincerest intention to wake up

Lightworkers to their true calling to heal the world.

Behold the veils are lifting!

May I shine the light and make a way for the new Earth!

Table of Contents

Part 1. The 10 Cosmic Dimensions

Introduction

A COLLABORATIVE WORK

This book is inspired by my clients asking, "How do I speak with my angels?" Humans are at different dimensions of spiritual evolution. Everyone evolves according to their intentions. This guidebook is meant as a road map to assist the spiritual aspirant in evaluating their strengths. It assists the spiritual aspirant to focus on areas of weakness for accelerated growth. In order to speak with your angels and Masters, you must be evolved to the 6th dimension. This guidebook clearly defines what that means.

The book indicates one's level of spiritual consciousness and helps one gauge where others are. Understanding spiritual evolution is valuable when working in a mixed dimensional environment like Earth. As a therapist, I perceive someone with 2nd dimensional consciousness differently than someone in the 10th dimension.

I consider the information in this book to be a collaborative work. While I am the author of this material, I clarify that the introduction was written from my perspective. Chapters 1 through 10 and The Spiritual Guidebook to Ascension are channeled material from the Light Realms.

I did not go into trance to write this book. I am fully awake and conscious and in my awake stake. I am fully clairaudient and as I write the book, they stop me and adjust sentences. They let me know if I forgot any points they intended. Writing the work is very conversation-based. I give numbers and percentages in the book. Nothing in this book is made up. The information has been communicated to me.

One will notice there is a unique vocabulary for this book. Therefore I have included a Glossary of Terms. It was important for the Masters to use language that was unique to this generation. They did not want me to use Christian vocabulary nor make Christian references. God is referenced to as Divine Source, Jesus as Christ Consciousness and Heaven as the Light Realms.

One might notice that the language of the work is simple. Sentences are short. This is not my normal writing style. This is the style of the Masters. They prefer simple and uncomplicated language so that everyone can easily read and access the information.

I have been awoken in the morning on several occasions and asked to transcribe notes from a meeting that occurred the night before. Often I am like the secretary for the group. I humbly bow as a servant for this work.

The spirit of Christ Consciousness has reincarnated many times on Earth. If you hold a Master in your heart by **any** name, good for you, stay on your path. All Masters are Divine Source. All angels are Divine Source. A Master that teaches love, compassion, forgiveness and acceptance is one with love, light and joy.

At the conclusion of writing this book, my team of Masters informed me it was time to change my name to Raven Shamballa. I was caught off guard once again. I did not ask for a different name. It was given to me. When I asked why, I was told it was a symbol of my spiritual growth and new mission.

MY PSYCHIC AWAKENING

My entire life changed in December 2014 following surgery. A month into recovery, I came off pain medication. I started hearing a voice. A male voice told me I wasn't doing my practice right. I needed to clean up my mess, organize my life and spiritualize my tools.

The story of my psychic awakening is momentous and deserving of its own book. It was a wild ride. After years of spiritual study and hoping that one day I could hear my angels, all of a sudden I could communicate with non-physical entities. I was having conversations with angels, White Light Masters and galactics.

I could speak with my clients' angels and Masters. I could connect with Divine Source, or God. I could speak with departed loved ones and others that had crossed over to the other side. I found that as long as I meditated and kept my chakra system clear from negative energy, I could ask questions and receive answers. I had the ability to contact a diverse array of entities in the non-physical dimensions. I was amazed that I had been blessed with this gift. A mission was given to me. I would communicate information received from the Light Realms.

My new insight was difficult for my family. They didn't know whether or not I was crazy. It seemed to them that I had become psychotic. I knew this was not mental illness. I was channeling. I was asked to perform a series of purification rituals. I underwent a series of testing. Many months later, I am grounded, still psychic and through the entry phase of my spiritual awakening.

I am grounded and ascended at the same time. I meditate daily, and am continuing with my therapy practice and energy healing work. A bridge was built so I could cross over at will. I had studied psychic development for years. Looking back over my life, I made a steady ascent up the spiritual ladder of consciousness. Now I have arrived as a spiritual counselor, pranic healer and psychic medium.

WESTERN AND EASTERN SPIRITUAL STUDIES

I have studied metaphysics, spirituality, New Age thought and Christ Consciousness my entire life. My parents were Christian ministers and I had spent my childhood in church. In adolescence, the church betrayed my family. After that painful trauma, I decided I would never go to church again. At 18, I left for college and noticed that I still had a strong desire for spiritual connection.

My ethnicity is half East Indian so I decided to practice yoga to regain my spiritual connection. For two years I read books on the topic. I discovered **Be Here Now** by Ram Dass and **Autobiography of a Yogi** by Paramahansa Yogananda. In my early 20s, I met my first hatha yoga teacher and began to practice yoga as a physical exercise. In my mid-20s, I found the Ananda Yoga Community in Seattle, Washington. This deepened my spiritual understanding of yoga. I found joy in meditation and under the watchful gaze of Jesus and Babaji Krishna, my heart opened and I became a born- again yogi.

My spiritual studies continued throughout my 20s. I investigated New Age topics. I followed and learned from different gurus. I worked at a New Age book store and was exposed to many diverse world religions, healing practices, paranormal phenomena and contemporary metaphysical authors. My spiritual essence began to

outgrow my corporate job. I decided to return home, go back to graduate school and study Western psychology.

During graduate school, I learned the technical aspects of listening, diagnosing, assessing, creating treatment plans and completing clinical paperwork. I worked as a yoga teacher, Pilates teacher and gave Thai yoga massages to make some income.

I had fun, too. I got a second degree in art and painted abstract color form. It was a productive and challenging time in my life. There were hours of therapy internship and the state board exams. The challenge was that my spiritual pursuits were brushed aside to embrace the Western licensure process. Although I was uncomfortable and it felt like it would never end, I was exposed to many subcultures – meth addicts, people involved with Child Protective Services and low-income county mental health patients. I served foster youth and disabled adults. I worked a four-month summer program as a clinician in a psych ward.

As an energy healer and therapist working in these environments, I learned a lot about negative energy and the power of energy clearing and meditation to transform lives. Throughout the last 10 years of my counseling practice, I have seen people significantly improve, very quickly as they release blocked chakras and negative energies.

HYPNOSIS AND ASCENSION

Finally, I had passed the tests. I started private practice. Now, I could return to my original interests of healing work, yoga and spirituality. In my post-grad studies, I became interested in hypnosis and energy healing.

A friend had suggested to me, years ago, that if I ever studied hypnosis, I should learn from Dolores Cannon. I remembered I wrote her name on a post-it in my home office. Months went by. One day, an intuitive nudge caused me to look at the post-it. I wondered about her training. I looked her up online. She was giving a level one training in Los Angeles in six weeks. I found that she held training all over the world. This was her only West Coast training in the year 2011. I had to go. That experience shifted my life and my perception on everything.

The training with Dolores Cannon was an amazing adventure and worthy of its own short story. I purchased a few of her books. They opened my mind. They were transcripts of her hypnosis sessions. Her clients were having unbelievable experiences in hypnotic trance. They were exploring past-life regression, the astral realms and life on other planets. Then, she would take the client to the level of their Higherself. Their Higherself would speak to them offering sacred information. Answers came to the questions "What is my life purpose?", "Should I move or change my job?" and "How do I manage difficult personal relationships?"

I was in awe. I went to work that evening, script in hand. I hypnotized a roommate back at the hostel where I was boarding. He went right in and had an amazing experience. He contacted his Higherself. I was astonished. You mean humans could journey to other realms and receive this information? Are you kidding me? Not only that, Dolores had the spiritual gift to heal people physically. I was committed. I wanted to advance in this skill. I decided to integrate hypnosis into my work as a psychotherapist.

Information discussed at Dolores's training is the basis for this book. One of Dolores's major works is a book called **Three Waves of Volunteers and the New Earth**. This book was a profound game-changer in my reality. I was introduced to the concept of Ascension and 5th dimensional consciousness. In this book, many of her clients relayed the message that the human race is in the process of ascending to higher dimensions.

Prior to the training, I was driving my car and I asked out loud, "What am I doing here among these ruffians? I don't belong here in this evil, dark world. There must be some mistake. I am not like everyone else." I heard a voice which said, "We recruited you and you volunteered, stop complaining and get to work." This message came to me prior to my reading Dolores's book. I understood I was a volunteer, recruited from a higher dimension. I incarnated to assist humans during the ascension process.

I was a Light Worker, here to bring light to a dark realm. I would assist to raise the dimensional consciousness of the planet. I would heal myself, heal others and heal the Earth. I started to research the concept of 5th dimensionality and found there were other metaphysical teachers discussing the topic. I understood the Ascension to be a mass consciousness event. We weren't going to be physically leaving our bodies and ascending into the Light Realms, we would remain physical but spiritually awakened. Humans could lift the veil and have communication with the astral realms.

100 CHAKRAS AND PSYCHOLOGICAL PRANIC HEALING

While I was learning about hypnotherapies and past life regression, I intuitively started to explore chakra balancing. I positioned the pendulum on top of a person's chakras while they were lying on their back. The pendulum would respond. I understood the pendulum was reading the spin of the chakra. I listened to people's narrative as a psychotherapist. I started to understand the language of the pendulum and chakras in relationship to the narrative the person was experiencing.

As a yoga teacher, I gave chakra readings after class. This furthered my comprehension and understanding of reading the pendulum. I developed a method for chakra balancing. I noticed that if clients focused on a chakra and affirmed a positive affirmation, the chakra would open and release blocked negative energy.

During this time, I studied energy work and pranic healing. I started to comprehend the energy body and learned how to assist people in healing psychological blocks through energy work and meditation. I would put a person into hypnosis and explore energy healing and chakra balancing.

After I had my psychic awakening, I started asking detailed questions. Masters on my team were coaching me on what to do. My clients were seeing results. As long as they believed in a higher power and angels, they would heal. Even long-term mental illness would heal. Time for treatment was relatively short, 4 to 8 to 20 sessions, depending on the illness.

A message came from the Masters. They were not just clearing the seven chakras - there were 100 chakras. I started working to understanding what was happening during the energy session. This work has continued to grow over the years. **The 100 Chakra System** is the title of my 2nd book which discusses energy healing in detail.

THE 5th DIMENSION – WHAT ABOUT THE 4th?

For many months I thought about the dimensions I really wanted more detailed information about what it meant to be 3rd dimensional and what it meant to be 5th dimensional. I noticed that others were talking about the move from the 3rd dimension to the 5th dimension. But they would not discuss the 4th dimension. Obviously, there had to be some in-between phase which moves you from the 3rd to the 5th dimension. I never found the answer until I had my psychic awakening and asked these questions directly.

At the Dolores Cannon's Level One training, another student had asked if and when we were going to go 5th dimensional. The student wanted to know how we would know when we moved into the 5th dimension. Dolores gave a rather vague answer. She said something to the effect of, "Many of us have already moved into the 5th dimension and more will be following in the next few years. You will know when you've moved into the 5th dimension, because your life will start to flow very smoothly." She went on to explain, "People who are negative, or of lower-dimensional consciousness, will shift out of your life." She said it would feel subtle. Lower dimensional friends and family would fall away. You would not hear from them again and you wouldn't miss their presence.

One would find their life would be pleasant and feel wonderful. The things of Earth, low frequency distractions, would magically lose their appeal. If you went into a grocery store and saw gossip magazines, you wouldn't be interested in them. They would feel unreal and plastic to you.

This concept of becoming 5th dimensional resonated with me. I believed it. I wanted to know more about it. I continued my search. I studied different teachers to answer my questions. After my psychic abilities came in, I finally got answers to my questions.

The answers were coming directly from Light Realm Masters. I could ask as many questions as I wanted. I began to receive detailed information. Eventually, they asked me to collaborate with them to write this book on the 10 Cosmic Dimensions. Every day I am honored and amazed by my magical life experiences. Channeling White Light Masters with Confidence

It is very important to me that people understand that I am communicating with Masters from the Light Realms. They gave me a mission, to help wake people up, assist them to connect directly to their divine teams and to move all humans in the direction of a kinder, softer, more loving and compassionate species.

This is the story of how I was introduced to my angelic team. Although I was spiritual and strongly intuitive, I knew I was not psychic. A major Ascension shift occurred on 12/12/12, December 12, 2012. I become more intuitive. I was seeing 11/11, but after 12/12/12, it changed to 444. I believed 444 meant that angels were watching over me and I shifted into the 5th dimension.

I was drawing angel cards as a divination tool. I knew angels were speaking to me. Over the years, I would channel personal messages. I didn't know who I was communicating with. I assumed it was one of my angels.

Before my psychic awakening, I performed past-life regression with clients. One of them told me a shaman

woman was visiting and I should meet her. The shaman was interested in hypnosis, but was looking for a qualified spiritual facilitator. I agreed to visit their guest and was curious to meet her.

She was trained by Native American Indians. At that time, my understanding of energy work was minimal. I didn't understand the shamanic tradition. She was trained in this approach. She asked me if I was working with guides and I said, "I thought so". I told her I believed I was surrounded by angels. But it was only an intuition. I couldn't say with certainty who I worked with.

I told the shaman this story: I was leading hypnosis, but the client wasn't going into a deep trance state. I started to panic. I wondered if the client would go under. The client kept saying, "I am walking in a forest and not arriving anywhere." This went on for some time. I was getting frustrated. I tried all the tricks I knew.

Finally, in desperation, I prayed, "Help me. What should I do next?" A female voice came to me and took over the hypnosis session. I was channeling her vibration. She restarted the script. As she went forward, I could see what the client was visualizing. For the first time I was clairvoyant.

That had never occurred to me before. The session went on and was successful. Before the voice left me, I asked for her name and she said it was Ashtara. I was quite proud of sharing this story. It was my first real contact with a spirit entity.

Then, the shaman questioned me further. "Did you ask where she was from?" It had not occurred to me to ask. I assumed she was an angel. She presented because I prayed for help. The Shaman asked me if I could tell her anything else about this guide. I told her she had an English accent and was a loving, jovial vibration.

At that point the shaman said, "I'm unable to work with you." She explained that there are many entities in the non-physical dimensions; some come from God, some come from the sky and many come from dark and evil places. She explained channeling was tricky and if I was working with non-physical beings, I should know with confidence exactly whom I was working with. That realization changed my perspective.

I completely respected her position. I walked away from the meeting feeling she was correct. I didn't know who my guides were, what their names were or where they came from. I trusted in myself and the knowingness of my own white light essence. I had years of spiritual practice. I believed that whatever was coming was coming to me from Heaven and God. I wasn't absolutely certain. I was operating on faith.

This meeting brought profound clarity. If I was working with guides, I should know who they were and where they came from. I prayed that I would advance and be worthy of knowing. Over the next couple of years, I continued to do past-life regression. I had interesting adventures in the non-physical dimensions. I continued to have faith. I prayed I would advance to know about my spiritual guides.

Then my psychic awakening occurred. As I came back to center, I heard the voice of Ki, an aboriginal shaman. Ashtara came in loud and clear. So did Big Bear, a Native American tribal and spiritual leader. The voices began and I could communicate with them. Now I could start asking questions.

"Who are you? What is your name? Where do you come from? What is your purpose? Why do you want to speak to me?" They would answer me. I could get detailed information. I received answers about my work, my practice, who exactly was on my team, what their names were and why they were assigned to me.

I had teams of angels working with me. Several Masters were instructing me and guiding my path. On a side note, I had been following the UFO community for the last 10 years out of curiosity. I was a regular listener to channeled messages. As my ability to channel grew, I was introduced to galactics orbiting in our solar system.

In the future, I plan to write about the events of my psychic awakening. For those who are curious, I published a five series Podcast on YouTube to tell some of the story. The point of this section is that I now know exactly who I am communicating with. I know where they come from and what subjects they are instructing. All come from love. All are aspects of Divine Source.

Chapter 1. The Golden Age

THE PURPOSE OF THIS WORK

We are moving into the Golden Age. As humans advance in Cosmic Consciousness, we will have the ability to directly connect to the Light Realms. The purpose of this work is to help people gauge where they believe they rank in the Cosmic Dimensions.

This helps the spiritual practitioner understand how to advance in spiritual consciousness and how to get to the next step. Lightworkers are humans who are 5th dimensional or higher. Humans are currently moving through the Ascension process. The Ascension process is pushing all humans towards the 5th dimension.

When I ask the Masters, "What is a client's dimensional consciousness?" I am presented with an average. For example, a client might be 6th moving to the 7th dimension. Then I ask, if this person could overcome their obstacles, what dimension would they be? They move up on the scale and most often, significantly. The person that overcomes their weakness then ranks at the 10th dimension.

This is motivating. It gives the client an idea of what they need to work on to accelerate in their spiritual growth. Many psychic development clients would really like to advance. This requires they meet the criteria of 5th dimensional consciousness.

Sometimes, the Masters will give me a number and it doesn't make sense based on the interview, as the client seems to be at a higher consciousness. Then I am told, "This is the dimension where they are stuck and they are unable to progress until they resolve an issue."

For example, one time I had a client with a strong devotional practice to Divine Source. He ranked low on the Cosmic Dimensional scale. This was because he held anger towards humanity. He had road rage and felt disrespected by rude people. The aspect of having a non-forgiving and non-compassionate stance lowered his overall dimensional consciousness. The practice of loving humanity and showing compassion regardless of other's behaviors would result in a higher dimensional consciousness.

This spiritual guidebook raises awareness and shows where the client needs to place their attention to move forward. A client might need to release childhood trauma. If they are holding anger and haven't forgiven family members, these negative energies impede spiritual growth. If you want to be a healer or a helper and cultivate your spiritual intuitions and gifts, you have to resolve past hurts. When these criteria are met one ascends to the next dimension.

Psychic development clients want more connection with the Light Realms. They want to advance in psychic gifts. They want to know why, after years of meditation, they don't seem to have intuitions or psychic awareness. My response is, you are asking to be 6th dimension, have you done the work of healing yourself? Each Cosmic Dimension has 11 steps. One can go through the steps to understand what they have accomplished and where they need to progress.

Spiritual evolution is a process, a journey. You don't just arrive at the 6th dimension without spiritual practice. This spiritual guide book offers specific information. One can know exactly what one needs to do to advance.

When people ask me about talking to their angels, I always ask, "What's your relationship with God?" A client might say, "Well, I believe in a higher power, or the universe, but I don't know exactly." I help them to clarify that the angels and Divine Source are of the same energy. If you want to be in relationship with angels then it's important that you feel connected to Divine Source.

Some children are born at an advanced level of dimensional consciousness. This is because they have done the spiritual work in other lifetimes and have cleared karmic residue. They are born gifted with spiritual skills. Other people are high in dimensional consciousness, but their conscious mind has not caught up to the spiritual dimension. As they become conscious of the concepts in this work, they quickly wake up and accelerate.

The reader will notice as they go through the guide book that the 4th and 5th dimensions have part 1 and part 2 phases. Humans spend a lot of time in the 4th and 5th dimensions because it takes time to heal and grow spiritually. The 4th and 5th dimensions are broken down into phases, so one can understand the progression of spiritual evolution.

MOVING UP AND DOWN
IN DIMENSIONAL CONSCIOUSNESS

Humans move up and down in dimensional consciousness. One can move into the 10th dimension while meditating with a teacher. After they leave the spiritual space, they go back to regular life. A job they don't like or a relationship that needs to end causes negative energy. They lower in spiritual consciousness again.

One can be 10th dimensional in nature, but when entering a city feel overwhelmed with negative energy. They don't understand how to hold their high dimensional state in a lower dimensional environment. They are unconsciously taking in the energy of others and lowering in dimension. They need tools to clear themselves.

The higher up in dimensional consciousness you go, the better you feel. The spiritual aspirant is motivated to stay high in consciousness. Dimensional consciousness rises or falls based on environment, family and friends, work and public spaces, the health of body and mind and spiritual practice.

Humans are highly affected by environments. Environments have spiritual dimensions. A spiritual place where people spend time devoted to Divine Source will have a high dimension. One will feel uplifted when entering the room. Likewise, if one walks into a bar, their dimension will lower.

Family and friends affect your energy level. If one lives with a depressed person, their energy can bring one down, if one allows it. Likewise, some families have negative habits. Families might complain, gossip, focus on negativity or pick fights. A significant other at a lower dimension will affect one because couples share the same auric field. Work environments and public spaces have dimensional consciousness. Most corporate and government jobs rank below the 2nd dimension. They are focused on money and put profits ahead of people. Businesses that give back to their communities hold a higher dimension. Public spaces are often polluted with negative energy. A Light Worker will feel the lower consciousness. They must decide if they want to exist in the environment or change their direction.

Diet affects our dimensional consciousness. There are high consciousness foods that come from Divine Source. Organic fruits and vegetables, lean meats, whole grains and water raise consciousness. Man-made foods like sugar, processed foods, deep fried food and junk foods lower one's consciousness. Alcohol and drugs open your energy body to negative energies that clutter your chakra system and create chaos in your life.

Thought patterns can raise and lower dimensions. Examine your thoughts and remove worry and fear-based thinking. Meditation disciplines your mind. The energy body needs to be cleared of all negative energy. A high consciousness Light Worker knows meditation will release everything foreign in their energy system.

Spiritual practice and exercise raise your dimensional consciousness. Meditation, yoga, healing work, and spiritual workshops will uplift consciousness, while a lack of focus on spiritual concerns will attach one to the material world of pain, suffering and endless desires.

To assist clients in understanding the dimensions of environment, family and friends, work and public spaces, I use a scaling system from 1 to 5. 1 on the scale means it's negative. 2 means lost and confused and has no heart. 3 means it has taken the first steps in the direction of light and healing. 4 means it's a heartfelt situation. And 5 means it's 5th dimensional and full of Christ Consciousness energy.

Conceptualizing the elements in your reality on a scale from 1 to 5 can help you understand what brings one up in consciousness and what brings one down.

All Lightworkers make choices about what they create in their reality. With strong intention, one creates a high dimensional reality. One finds themselves surrounded with high dimensional people, environments and good work. Every day is a good day.

THE COSMIC RAY

Humans are assisted in the Ascension process by an energy current called the Cosmic Ray. The Cosmic Ray is known by several other names on the Internet. The concept is that Divine Source is sending an energy wave from the Light Realms to assist with raising dimensional consciousness. All humans and especially Lightworkers are affected by the Cosmic Ray.

The Cosmic Ray ebbs and flows like the tide. The Cosmic Ray showers the planet with varying waves of intensity. The higher the intensity of the ray, the more positive energy is in the atmosphere. The ray, in conjunction with astrological alignments, has produced phenomenal advancements in human consciousness. The Cosmic Ray started affecting humanity in 2009 and will continue to push human consciousness in the direction of Ascension over the next 50 years.

....

The Cosmic Ray is measured on a scale from 1 to 10. 10 is considered the maximum intensity. The intensity reaches 10 on the scale three to four times a year. As the wave hits our atmosphere, the energy pushes human consciousness forward.

....

When the ray is at 10 intensity, Lightworkers move up in dimensional consciousness, literally overnight. The shift can be subtle or dramatic. A Light Worker may have feelings to leave a job or relationship. A new spiritual teacher comes in to advance their practice. Lightworkers might find they have stronger psychic skills or discover new spiritual gifts.

Some Lightworkers experience Ascension symptoms. Ascension symptoms include headaches, fatigue and withdrawal from the world. They may feel dizziness or a feeling of floating. Lightworkers are adjusting to new levels in consciousness. After the maximum intensity of the Cosmic Ray passes, they feel normal but changed.

The 5 Aspects of a person (physical, mental, emotional, energetic and spiritual) are literally shifted. This is happening at a consciousness level, but also happens on all levels. For example, one decides to buy organic and use natural medicine instead of pharmaceutical medication. One decides to shop at a health food store instead of a corporate store. One decides it's time to resolve hurt feelings from childhood. We are inspired to meditate or become healers. One learns about crystals, herbs, sound healing and hypnosis. There are countless examples of subtle shifts in our consciousness that are progressively moving us forward in dimensional consciousness.

5th COSMIC DIMENSION VERSUS 5th DENSITY

After I channeled the 10 Cosmic Dimensions, I asked a question. "Is this the same idea as 5th Density?" I follow channeled messages on the Internet. Many people are channels for angels, Masters and galactics. Galactics are high-dimensional beings from other locations in the Astrodome or the universe. Galactics are already 5th Density or higher and are assisting humans with the Ascension process.

Channeled messages referenced 5th density and 5th dimensional to described our nest goal point to reach in human consciousness. These two words have the same meaning. Authors using the terminology 5th density or 5th dimensional relay the same messages. Humans are ascending and will become 5th density or 5th dimensional.

I wanted to clarify the two different scales. In this book, I write on the 10 Cosmic Dimensions. This scale measures the spiritual evolution of a human. The Cosmic Dimension scale goes from -1 up to 30. This book defines dimensions -1 to 10. This Cosmic Dimension scale is measuring love, healing, health, and comprehension of spiritual concepts like working with angels, multi-dimensions and dreamtime.

The Density scale refers to spiritual evolution and also physical density. The higher you go in spiritual understanding, the lighter your physical density becomes. A high dimensional soul eats a pure diet to stay light and keep the weight off. When you eat light, it is easier to meditate. Lightness of being feels expansive, open and free.

The Density and Cosmic Dimension scales are related but different. Density refers to physical and spiritual lightness. It's a reference to the Light Body or Lightbody. Souls that have a high density are profoundly spiritual but still retain a physical form. Density is the measurement of the physical form. Cosmic dimensions are referring to human spirituality only.

Galactics are of different densities. Humans are galactics because we have physical form. Some galactics are so light that we can't perceive them with our physical eyes or current technologies. Angels are not galactic. They are considered astral; they have no physical form. They have the ability to take a form for specific purpose, to interact with humans, but are considered astral.

On the Cosmic Dimensional scale, the hope is that all humans will ascend to the 5th dimension or higher. In this regard, many of us have already ascended and will continue to ascend as we move into higher dimensions.

Authors who speak of the density state explain that humans will move into the 5th density. As we become more spiritual, we will become physically lighter.

> **To date, most of the human race is 3rd density. About 25% of humans are 3rd moving to the 4th density. They are becoming physically lighter, and their DNA is shifting. Less than 5% are 4th density. In 2016, there were no humans at the 5th density. This will change as our human spiritual evolution accelerates and we move into 2019.**

To illustrate, a person might be ascended to the 10th Cosmic Dimension, but physically they are 3rd density. As humans continue to ascend in spiritual consciousness, we will continue to lighten physically. Once we enter the 15th cosmic dimension or higher, we are in the 3rd density moving to the 4th density. When we cross into the 25th dimension, we are 4th density. When we cross into the 50th spiritual dimension, we are 5th density. At that point you might consider that the scales merge. The galactics that are assisting in human evolution are 5th to 10th density or higher.

THE SHIFT AWAY FROM RELIGION TO A UNIQUE SPIRITUAL PATH

In order to move up in dimensional consciousness, we have to connect to Divine Source. Humans are confused about how to connect to Divine Source, the Masters and angels. This is because we are evolving into a new consciousness where we will access Divine Source directly. Formal religion is beneficial if one is spiritually growing and experiencing joy. The modern-day church has limitations, confusions and inconsistencies.

Historically, humans have relied on religion to show us the way to Divine Source. Religion gave us ceremony, spiritual community, a defined moral code and spiritual practice. All of that is valid. What has changed is our dimensional consciousness. Religion has become impersonal, watered down and limited in spiritual growth. Many believe in Divine Source or a higher power but are not interested in going to church.

Most of us are not interested in church because we just don't feel joy. Spirituality needs to move from church on Sunday to a spiritual practice that allows us to experience Divine Source daily. Everyone needs to find a personal way to connect to Divine Source.

When connected, one's life and relationships are full of love. One feels positive and upbeat. One understands their life purpose. One brings positive change to the world. We understand forgiveness and karma. We have a strong moral code and integrity. One feels caring, joyful and abundant. Our path needs to be meaningful and real to us.

> **5th dimensional consciousness means one is healed on all levels of their being. One has embraced Christ Consciousness. To all Beings everywhere, love and compassion. There are no boundaries, there are no nations and we are all one.**

What is important is that one finds a personal way to connect to Divine Source. Individually, each of us will find our own spirituality. Many of us will create or find spiritual communities. We will ascend into joy. Our lives transform because we have a direct connection. We feel the higher vibrations of love, light and joy. We move away from anger and fear. Spiritual gifts open. We are healed. We are able to heal others and heal the world.

Chapter 2. Love, Compassion, Forgiveness and Acceptance

The first step in the cosmic dimension guidebook is Love, Compassion, Forgiveness and Acceptance.

This is our primary work in physicality. Humans are here to learn and understand this truth. It cleanses our essence and returns us to Divine Source. Earth is a free-will and free-choice planet, mixed together with dark energies that seek to confuse and anger. There are billions of dramas that play out. We are free to do what we choose and are separate from Divine Source. This is both a blessing and a curse.

We should hold the intention to reconnect on our journey. If we do not find our way to the light, we can get lost and suffer greatly. Love is at the core of this teaching. The Earth plane is oriented to the darker energies. We are removed from holy places and practices. Our world play is based on survival and scarcity of resources. This sets up a reality of confusion and despair.

Dark energies are all around us. We have to consistently stay clear and avoid them. This can be a difficult task if one is ready to grow on the Cosmic Dimensional scale. In order to reconnect, we have to invite the light into our life and avoid darkness. Light energies must be requested, while dark energy consistently invades. Our world is charged toward the negative. Remaining pure requires extra effort on our part.

Light energies have to be invited into our auric fields. We have to make an effort. We need to find a spiritual practice that works for us. We have to request angels and Masters to guide us and come to our aid. Dark energies will play their part to dissuade us. The influence of the dark is around every corner. We can easily become lost and confused. We are baited to stay entrapped until such time as we are grounded in our truth.

Christ Consciousness is the teaching of love, compassion, forgiveness and acceptance. Once we are conscious of this truth, we start to practice these attitudes. More love comes into the Lightbody. This allows us to connect to God and to our Higherself.

Our life purpose is known by the Higherself. When we are on our spiritual path we understand our life purpose. We feel good and have the capacity to enjoy our life to the fullest. When there is love in our life, we are more fulfilled. To the contrary, when we feel stalled on our path, we become lost and confused. We don't understand what life is about, why we play this game or why we incarnated.

Your belief about love, compassion, forgiveness and acceptance determines the quality of your reality. You have to believe that you come from a place of love and eventually will return to that eternal place. You have to know that all will be forgiven. You have to understand compassion is endowed to all. Divine Source, the Masters, even the dark energies all understand the constructs of the game. You must learn to feel for love and joy. You have to want to hold love in every aspect of your life. When you feel blocked, you have to take action to center and reconnect to love.

The start of growth in cosmic consciousness is to love yourself. Within all of us, there is a spark of divine light. Once we are conscious of that light, we can expand it. For some of us, this is a hard task. You start by being your own best friend. You have to have compassion for your journey. You have to forgive yourself for any past mistakes, conscious or unconscious. You have to forgive yourself and move forward with more wisdom and determination to move on.

Practicing forgiveness means letting go of anger. All of us have lots of story line and narrative. No one is perfect and all have made wrong choices. Even if you think you have done fairly well in this present consciousness at your soul essence, there is a lot more story line. That's okay. It's a set up. That is the play of the drama of separation from God. First, we fall and eventually we land and discover. When we are ready, we surrender and we look up to the light.

The act of surrender moves us into acceptance. We need to accept our likes and dislikes, our triumphs and defeats. We accept our childhood dramas, we overcome the karma that we were born into. We surrender into who we are and what we agreed to do. We accept what we cannot change or what we don't have control over. We only hold responsibility for ourselves and our journey. We allow everyone the same freedom that Divine Source has given us to journey and find our way home. The key is love and it starts with loving yourself.

THE CORE OF THE TEACHING

Love, compassion, forgiveness and acceptance are the core teachings of this work.

Practicing these attitudes is what moves one forward in the cosmic dimensions. We recognize that all love comes from Divine Source and that all are part of it. We appreciate Divine Source, for without consciousness and separation we could not partake in this reality.

When we become angry at God, we have lost our way. We will quickly lose our direction. We cannot orient to the light. Some of us become angry at God due to our karma. We focus on our suffering. We need to practice compassion and we need to love Divine Source regardless. This is the only way out of darkness. We are not conscious of the reason for our story. We can only hope that love will guide our way and find us eventually in peace.

Next, we love ourselves. We believe we can create the very best reality. We believe we deserve a wonderful life. We leave behind all the people and situations that don't serve our greatest good. Then we practice loving others. Loving others is a broad category. Like concentric circles, we start with our innermost ring. We master loving people in our family and our significant others. We figure out how to be in healthy relationships.

If our families have been healthy, it is easy to appreciate them. But if our families have been hurtful, some of us need to distance ourselves to heal. Depending on our capacity to love, some only love a few. They never move past feeling love for their intimate circles. Others appreciate many beyond their innermost ring. Love is the process of giving and receiving. The more love we give, the more love we receive.

As people expand in consciousness, they move to the next ring of loving their communities. For some, this comes naturally. They want to help. They are aware that their neighbors and the people they see in their community all contain the divine spark of God-source energy. For others, there are just too many rude and disrespectful people. Everyone seems cold and cut off. For those people who hold generalized anger towards others, this is their spiritual work; to grow in love of others, whether they are conscious of it or not.

The next ring of love is humanity. We love those we do not know. We love all beings everywhere. This is the truest expression of Christ Consciousness: to all beings everywhere, love and compassion. We don't have to know them personally to love them deeply. When we arrive at this consciousness, we are expanding in dimensional consciousness.

Gaia is the spiritual name of Earth. Gaia's animals and all the wonderful species of life become avenues through which to transmit our love. We honor Gaia as she provides the structure and container in which we play. As this consciousness grows, we choose to be of no harm to Gaia and her inhabitants. We are gentle and kind. We walk softly and become more conscious of the footprints we leave behind.

Compassion means, 'I love you no matter what.' The parent-child relationship is the most compassionate relationship humans know. When the baby comes to the mother, it only knows that it loves that mother. Most mothers love their children, regardless of their hurtful ways or disabilities. Parents love their children, no matter what. This idea of compassion is programmed into our being.

When we grow in cosmic consciousness, our compassion expands. I am willing to love you no matter what, even if I don't know you, even if I can't understand your suffering, even if you are hurtful and mean. This is the hardest lesson of love, to embrace and to forgive the dark enemies.

Compassion and forgiveness go hand in hand. Forgiveness means I release all the hurt that you have given me. Forgiveness means you become neutral to pain and no longer wish to perpetuate the cycle of anger. Forgiveness means you love them enough to let go of their bad behavior and see it as their lesson from which to grow. Forgiveness is the willingness to let go of anger quickly. The sooner we forgive, the sooner we move back into love.

There is an understanding in the astral realm that this reality is very challenging. Many of us can easily get lost. Divine Source, which created all, is most aware of this and therefore all is forgiven. At the end of the play, it is important to feel worthy and loved by God. This ensures that we will return to Divine Source. There is still the justice system of karma, but all is forgiven. We continue to walk the Earth realm and play the game until the lessons are learned.

Our soulful essence is born into a body, a location, a family and deals with the reality that governs the situation. We take what we were given, and we work with it. Oftentimes, there are aspects of our creation that we cannot change. Acceptance means we give up all resistance to those aspects we have no control over. This can be an unforeseen event, a sickness that presents, the loss of a loved one and countless other obstacles that require acceptance.

Love, compassion, forgiveness and acceptance are the fundamental building blocks to growing in dimensional consciousness. Ultimately, this is why we came to Earth; to experience, learn and practice these attitudes. The contrary attitudes of anger, suffering, depression and apathy keep us in bondage to uncomfortable and dark realities. Our work is to practice these attitudes and expand them to all beings everywhere.

THE JOURNEY INTO THE HEART

The journey into the heart is finding our way from darkness into light. There are varying degrees of darkness and there are varying degrees of light. Where you are born and what you are trying to achieve in terms of dimensional consciousness is unique for each individual. If a person's consciousness falls in the lower dimensions, they are unaware of the light. If one is lost and confused, they are aware of Divine Source and unconcerned with spiritual advancement. And, if one is in the growth dimensions or higher dimensions, they are aware of the light and seek more joy in their life.

Each time we are born, we start from scratch. We have amnesia. The task is to remember who one is, where one came from and what one is trying to learn in this lifetime. If we have made progress on our journey, we are placed in a more supportive role for spiritual advancement. And if we have been lost in darkness, there is less support, and self-motivation to find the light becomes the primary concern.

In the lower dimensions, a person is lacking in love and feels great pain and suffering. Often times, this person has been hurt or abandoned by their family. They feel wounded. Deep-seated anger can keep the person locked in a cycle of fear and hopelessness. They are angry at the world around them. Lack of love may cause a person to seek a substitute for true love. They find themselves in abusive relationships and suffering from addictions. Low self-esteem and an unwillingness to forgive keeps them locked in anger and resentment.

Sometimes it takes hitting rock bottom to turn toward self-reflection and to ask for help. This is part of the process of growth. A person may survive a suicide attempt or lose everything due to addiction. A soul may call out for rescue out of desperation. Sometimes people don't wake up. They fail in their mission. They stay lost and confused, cycling around in darkness. This is allowed by Divine Source. Each soul is granted the opportunity to arrive at their own ideal pace. In the lower dimensions, most people are learning through the experience of drama and trauma.

Many people are lost and confused. They believe, or want to believe, in Divine Source but don't feel the presence of joy in their lives. They become disconnected and don't understand how to reconnect. Church can play the role of providing spiritual guidance. But in this age, many feel that the church has been compromised, or they don't resonate with the message. Many have been wounded by the church or feel it is too much about money. Many people raised in the church don't take their children to services. As a result, it is up to us individually to make the effort to find a personal way to connect to love, light and joy.

Contemplation of spirituality, our soul bodies and the afterlife are often tuned out. Contemplation for many comes only at a point of despair, such as the death of a loved one. And even then, it is easy to dismiss this contemplation and go back to normal everyday life. Lack of spiritual consciousness has produced a dark world. If you are a good person, but unaware of the light, it is easy to have a weak moral code. It is easy to favor money over humanity. It is easy to get lost on your journey. And most importantly, there is a lack of joy and a disconnection from the light. This causes despair and confusion, suffering and pain.

ASCENSION TO THE 5th DIMENSION AND BEYOND

In the growth dimensions, we spend most of our time trying to master the concepts of love, compassion, forgiveness and acceptance. We desire to move in the direction of love and compassion for ourselves and others. We have to work to heal and work to forgive. We have to find what brings us joy. We have to find our passion. We have to make decisions in alignment with our heart. We have to connect to our Higherself. We need to find our purpose and complete our mission.

Then we have to ask for forgiveness. Forgiveness is necessary to move away from anger and toward love. If we are unwilling to forgive, we harbor anger and this sabotages love. We have to consciously choose love instead of fear. As we release negative emotions, we feel more love. We move from a place of disconnection to feeling at one with everything. Love and anger do not exist in the same heart space. Forgiveness allows love to move forward. You have to forgive yourself, others, your family, your community and your world.

Next, we progress to a point where we ask forgiveness from God and the Masters. We become aware of our shortcomings. We understand the context of the play. We see how karma works. One desires forgiveness, so they can progress. We waste no time stating, "I am sorry. Please forgive me." We desire that all the dark be taken away, because we understand it brings us despair. We want more light because we understand it brings us joy.

As you ascend higher in cosmic consciousness, you become aware of the astral realm. In order to progress, a person must take a Master to guide their path. Most people will consciously take a Master through their spiritual practice. Some people unconsciously are born with a Master in their heart. They haven't had much spiritual orientation in this lifetime and yet they are guided in the direction of their growth. Other times, a person just believes in God as an abstract concept of light that is in all people. They may start the practice of meditation. Whether they are conscious of it or not, a Master has come into their heart.

A Master is important because they guide one on their journey. They understand the why behind your incarnation. They understand the lessons the soul is trying to get out of the experience. A Master will also assist one in resolving karma for time spent in darkness. For some of us, the concept of the Master is profound. We rely heavily on their blessings and guidance. For others, the concept of the Master is less important. What is important is that we hold the consciousness that we are never alone. As we intend to progress in our spiritual evolution, we are supported by guides who light the way.

Spiritual practice is the next phase of evolution. We choose an activity and spiritualize it. We devote that activity to growing in the direction of love. Spiritual practice brings one joy. It should not feel like a chore. One's spiritual practice reconnects them to their center. The more time spent in spiritual practice, the faster one grows in cosmic consciousness. If it is our intention, psychic gifts and spiritual powers awaken. We can unlock sacred truths and become healers. As you ascend, you want to be surrounded by love. This includes the people in your intimate circle, your work environment and spiritual community. This can be challenging for the spiritual aspirant as they start to grow out of unhealthy relationships and difficult work environments. Priorities shift and change is required. One wants all aspects of their life to radiate in 5th dimension consciousness. This includes our family and friends, our activities, our food choices and especially our work.

Occupations are especially challenging as one moves up in dimensional consciousness. One becomes inspired to do meaningful work and be of service. As one heals, they may be called to be a healer or a helper. This can mean leaving low dimension occupations where money is valued over the heart. Sometimes as one shifts up in consciousness, others at lower dimensions can't relate. One might be targeted due to one's unwillingness to participate in petty concerns and gossip.

Once a person has done the growth work and defined spirituality for themselves, they will quickly progress in dimensional consciousness. They find themselves healthy and healed. They are grounded in a spiritual practice and no longer attracted to lower dimensions, people and activities. They become qualified to assist others. They find themselves in the 5th dimension. Happy, healed, in the moment and at peace with all that is.

The higher frequency dimensions are available for our enjoyment. Spiritual gifts and psychic awakenings can develop if the spiritual aspirant desires. The bridge to the higher dimensions and the astral realms is crossed. What once seemed a far away and distant concept becomes as real as this temporary and fragile reality. Wisdom and insight are gained and shared. Joy becomes the primary expression of one's life.

In the higher dimensions, every day feels good. There is no running from anything, no avoiding pain. There is just a relaxed and happy quality of being. If stress or tension comes, there is an understanding of how to breathe, get back to center and release whatever it is that is distracting one from feeling the joy. There is no fear. The temporal aspects of this reality are understood. All is well, and love, compassion, forgiveness and acceptance are fully embraced and practiced in all aspects of every moment of every day.

Chapter 3. The Five Aspects of Yourself

The second step of the Cosmic Dimensions is called the Five Aspects of Yourself. This step covers healing on all levels of your being. You have five aspects: your physical body, your mental body, your emotional body, your energy body and your soulful body. When all five aspects are in balance, you are functioning at an optimal level.

PHYSICAL BODY

These five aspects together make up your being. We are most identified with our physical form. We can see it. We can understand its history. We know its ethnicity and DNA lineage. It is the vehicle through which we express our soulful essence. It is our mechanism for experience. Through our brain and five senses we exist in the physical dimension.

Our physical body is an indicator for measuring our overall health.

The health of our lungs and our ability to breathe are directly related to our quality of life. Our muscular strength reflects our ability to be strong and confident. Our self-confidence is related to the appearance of our physical form. When our vehicle is healthy, we have the ability to excel in our life purpose as healers and helpers. When our vehicle is sick, we have an opportunity to grow in understanding how to heal ourselves.

MENTAL BODY

Our mental body is called our intellect. In many wisdom teachings, it is also called our ego. It is that aspect of our consciousness that thinks, plans and creates strategies. It calculates, problem-solves, and reads maps. It learns and follows directions. It contains our conscious memory and the history of our present lifetime. The mind perceives three dimensions of time: past, present and future. It can perceive the past as successful or as a failure. It can imagine outcomes in the future as either positive or negative. This linear landscape allows for record keeping, growth and evaluation. It allows us to learn our life lessons.

The consciousness of the mental body is limited. This is on purpose by Divine design. We are made to have amnesia before we are born. We start from scratch each time. We play the game of physicality and perceive it as the ultimate reality since we don't have any recollection of where we came from. Our soulful résumés are full of pain, suffering, victories and pleasures. Knowing our soulful history would alter the way we perceive the game.

Because we are in physicality, our mind perceives the physical world as the only reality. Non-physical realities are immeasurable in physicality. Masters that perceive beyond this dimension teach that the non-physical dimensions are real. Humans are asked to have faith that they are real, even though most of us cannot perceive them. As we shift up in dimensional consciousness, we can perceive the non-physical dimensions.

Our mental body dictates the personality of ourselves. It contains our likes and dislikes. It contains our desires and the directions we move toward. Our mind is programmed with our life purpose. This is why some of us climb mountains and others prefer the safety of home. The programming inside influences our choices.

Our mental body creates thoughts. Our thoughts are very powerful. Our thoughts create our reality. We steer the course of our life story based on our intentions. Our intentions determine how we perceive our reality.

A thought is non-physical. A seed thought is an idea. A non-physical thought produces an action and that action brings into play our desired outcomes in physicality.

EMOTIONAL BODY

Our ability to feel comes from the emotional body. Much like thoughts, our emotions are abstract and non-physical. They register in our physical body as sensations, tears or tight muscles. We cannot see them. We experience them.

The human experience allows for a wide range of positive and negative emotions. Typically, we enjoy the positive emotions and prefer not to feel the negative ones. Therefore, our emotions are subjective. We have likes and dislikes. We like the feeling of love, but dislike the feeling of pain.

We prefer the feelings that are generated from love. Joy, peace, calmness, gentleness, feeling proud and feeling carefree all come from Divine Source. We prefer not to experience the feelings that come from fear. Anger, depression, shame, boredom and jealousy all originate from fear.

As humans, we feel a range of positive and negative emotions. We experience obstacles and challenges. We react to situations. Our emotional response depends on how we perceive reality. We are triggered by other people or live through calamities and unforeseen events. All of this is an experiment to observe our emotional control.

As we grow and mature, we learn to not overreact emotionally.

Emotions enhance our experience and make our reality feel real. Life is accented by our ability to feel. Emotions act as an antenna. We are motivated to feel joy, passion, enthusiasm and success. If the person or situation brings us a feeling of joy and expansion, we move in that direction. If the person or situation makes us feel fear and anger, we should move in a different direction.

Uncomfortable emotions play the role of helping us grow in our understandings. Remorse, for example, assists one in feeling bad about their behavior. Grief is a testimony to love when there is loss. The goal is to center your emotions and attune to love. We learn to have faith that the outcome will ultimately be positive. We turn away from fear-based emotions and move in the direction of joy. Energy Body

The energy body is non-physical and exists in and around our physical body, like a double imprint. Like the emotional body, the energy body governs how we feel. Because the energy body is subtle and underlying, we are less aware of it.

The energy body is composed of energetic material. Some of us can see it clairvoyantly. Many of us can feel it energetically. This energy comes from Divine Source and you could consider that all material is composed of Divine Source energy. It is the life force and building block for all physicality. Underneath our physical form is energy.

Energy is known by other names in literature. In Indian traditions it is called prana, in Chinese traditions it is called chi and in Japan it is called ki. In the West, we say white light energy or the energy of the universe. In the Christian church, this energy is referred to as the Holy Spirit. All of these words refer to the same substance. It is Divine Source energy.

The energy body is also known as the astral body or the etheric body. It is energy based; you cannot touch or hold it like a material object. Like thoughts and feelings, it does not exist in the physical dimension. The energy body exists in the astral dimension, an energy realm.

Your energy body has a composition. It contains your inner and outer auric field, your chakra system, your meridians, your health rays and your center column of light. This divine line is also known in literature as the silver cord which connects you to Divine Source.

Your inner auric field is an inch around your physical body and most people can see it if they look for it. Your outer auric field is around the body at an arm's length and can expand and contract to make your auric field bigger or smaller.

Your chakra system is comprised of energy centers. The seven major centers are located on your center line but other minor chakras are located around the body. You also have chakras on your divine line numbering up to 100. These higher chakras are unknown in literature and too complex to describe here. What is important to know is that they contain karmic residue and, like the seven major chakras, can be activated and cleared.

Your meridians are channels that allow energy to flow around the body, in a similar fashion to veins that allow blood to move around the body. The meridian points can get blocked. Acupuncturists use needles to clear blocked meridian points. Blocked energy can appear as pain in the body.

Your health rays are like fine beams of light that radiate throughout your auric field. Your divine line is like a tube of light that extends downward into physicality and upward into Divine Source. If one is growing in dimensional consciousness, one is centered in the heart chakra. Our 100 chakras are aligned to our center column of light. Our spinal cord is our physical column. Our energetic divine line extends around our spinal cord. When Divine Light comes in, all of these elements are activated, and it animates our being and brings us joy.

Our emotional body and our energy body both hold emotions. We can release strong emotional feelings through the physical body. For example, when we cry, we are releasing the emotional feeling of sadness through the physical form of tears. Likewise, we can release sadness through the energy body. The feeling of sadness has an energetic form. Sadness can look like a dark cloud lodged in the heart chakra. If there is sadness in your heart, you can release this feeling energetically. An energy healer knows how to release the uncomfortable emotion out of the energy field.

When we are attuned to Divine Source energy, we have the ability to channel in love and joy. This energy activates our chakras and animates our physical form. When we have an abundance of energy, we feel good. When all of our chakras are open and f lowing, we function optimally.

THE LIGHTBODY

The soulful body, also called the Lightbody, or Higherself, is non-physical. It is our spiritual essence. It is referred to as the Lightbody because clairvoyant eyes would see it as glowing white light. It is energetic and consists of Divine Source energy. Both the energy body and Lightbody are composed of energetic material. The Lightbody is considered different from the energy body because it is permanent and infinite. The energetic body is temporal and finite and terminates when the physical body or incarnation ends.

The Lightbody is always present but is dormant. It awakens when the conscious mind acknowledges it is there. Once the ego is aware of the soul's essence, the ego can allow the Higherself to guide the temporal bodies for optimal growth and a positive experience.

The Lightbody is limitless. It is connected to Divine Source. Once a Lightbody is birthed from the Divine Source, it holds a boundary which allows it to experience as an individual cell. This allows for experience and relationship, growth and individuality. Some souls choose to merge back into Divine Source and other souls choose to participate in and observe creation.

The Lightbody is large compared to the physical body. In fact, the Lightbody has to compress itself to merge into the vehicle of the physical body. During meditation, the Lightbody has an opportunity to expand. This feels good to the soul's essence. It is freed to open and expand itself. This is also called an out-of-body experience.

....

The Lightbody is conscious of its soul's history. The Lightbody doesn't have amnesia. It is aware of all of its narratives. This lifetime is like one storybook. The conscious mind is the main character in the story. The Lightbody is the consciousness that has read several books on the bookshelf. It is aware of each main character it has ever played in its library of experience.

....

The Lightbody contains our soulful résumé. Even though our conscious mind may not remember prior experiences, our Higherself does. We each have a résumé of experience and can discover our gifts. Gifts are the result of prior knowledge studied in other experiences. We are skilled in certain areas because it is not the first time we have attempted it.

Our Lightbody holds our karmic record. We receive karma when we make mistakes. We are held responsible for our mistakes and must purify ourselves. Karma is a justice system. A record is maintained in the astral realm. The karmic experience of challenge is governed by the 100 chakras in our divine line. Each trauma or mistake presents as a block in the higher chakras. The spiritual aspirant should desire to clear their 100 chakras. The clearer your chakra system, the more light f lows through it. One's Lightbody shines through the physical vehicle with love and grace.

The Lightbody contains your life purpose, your life path and understands the reasons for your experience. It understands the goals of this lifetime. It has a general idea about what it would like to accomplish, what it would like to learn and what it needs to atone for. When we are on our life path, we intuitively know we are moving in the right direction. And when we fall off the path, we feel lost.

The Lightbody is attuned to divine wisdom. It understands about integrity and following the moral code. The soul is deeply aware of karmic consequences. It is always interested in connecting to the other temporal bodies and hopes the conscious mind will acknowledge its divine wisdom. When the conscious mind is unaware of its Higherself, the Higherself is in observation. It is watching the experience and not actively participating. Once the Higherself is acknowledged, it plays an integral role in guiding the conscious mind and the physical body to stay on course.

Your soul's history, your soul's résumé, your karmic record and your life purpose are all stored in the Lightbody. This information does not come forward unless one consciously decides to uncover it. Through the process of meditation, dreamtime and hypnosis, many people have found ways to access the Lightbody or Higherself.

The Lightbody can connect to and receive the energy from Divine Source. Our divine line connects directly to Divine Source. Through this cord, we can feel the emotional expressions of love, light and joy. When a personality becomes disconnected from Divine Source, it feels lost and confused. When we are connected to Divine Source, we feel joy. The clearer the channel, the greater the amount of joy.

The Higherself is often underutilized until the personality self-investigates. If the conscious mind is not listening for answers, it cannot hear the divine wisdom of its Higherself. Once the conscious mind is aware of its Higherself and starts to listen, the personality makes different choices and is guided in the direction it needs to go.

The Lightbody is that aspect of the self that can transcend physicality. It is important to take breaks from this reality as it is mixed dimensional and often uncomfortable. When we close our physical eyes, we move into the non-physical realities. This is why we close our eyes to pray or meditate. We are acknowledging communication with the non-physical or spiritual realms. Meditation is the experience of quieting the temporal aspects of yourself and bringing forward the infinite and expansive Lightbody.

HIERARCHY OF THE FIVE ASPECTS OF THE SELF

There is an optimal hierarchy for the five aspects of a person. Ideally, the Lightbody should be directing the physical, mental, energetic and emotional bodies. The Lightbody should be at the top of the pyramid and the other bodies should be in alignment at the bottom. When this occurs, your Higherself guides your reality. Your Higherself knows your life purpose, life path and life goals. It has a specific intention for what you are trying to accomplish.

Your Higherself is that aspect of you that is connected to Divine Source. It is part of Divine Source. It understands integrity and encourages a strong moral code. Your Higherself feels guilty when one makes a mistake. It knows it performed an action outside of integrity. Your Higherself understands why you are playing the game called life.

The Higherself ideally guides the physical, mental, energetic and emotional bodies when obstacles come up. The Higherself should direct the conscious mind and physical body. The mind and body will then understand how to best align themselves to the truth. The right actions would be taken because the Higherself wants to meet life goals according to one's purpose.

When we are disconnected from our Lightbody, one of the other bodies will take the lead in problem-solving, often resulting in an imbalance. If we have an emotional problem, like loneliness, the physical body may attempt to solve this problem. The physical body is good at digestion and this is one of the things it does best. Therefore, the physical body suggests that it can solve the problem by eating. If, at the soulful level, the person is missing sweetness, they may crave sugar. If they are missing excitement, they may crave chips and fun food. If they are lonely, they might eat continuously to avoid feeling alone. This is the root of emotional eating.

The mind also has a mechanism for problem-solving. The mind is good at thinking, planning, and coming up with potential outcomes. The issue is that the mind can overthink a situation, or dwell on negative outcomes. This often results in worrying. The mind will do what it is good at: thinking. And the mind will think and think and think, often causing the person to feel uncomfortable and move into a state of anxiety.

The Lightbody, on the other hand, would handle the situation differently. If the person felt alone, it would encourage itself to be brave and meet new people. If the person needs sweetness, the Higherself would encourage the person to move away from meanness and find company that was nice. If the person was bored, it might encourage a change in occupation or to create an adventure. The Lightbody would steer clear of negative people and environments. The Higherself would want the person to be healthy. It would move them toward fulfilment and away from distractions.

When we are disconnected from our Lightbody, we feel lost and wonder about our life purpose. We wonder what we are doing here. What am I trying to accomplish? We tend to get confused. When the physical body and mental body are in control, they tend to form imbalances. We become emotionally full of negative energy and experience depression and anxiety.

When we are aligned to our Higherself, we make better choices. We move our life in a positive direction. We feel passionate and motivated. We enjoy the process of our life unfolding as we are working in the direction of our goals. We move toward our greatest good and highest happiness.

THE FIVE ASPECTS RELATED TO THE COSMIC DIMENSIONS

As you move up in dimensional consciousness, you become more conscious of the Five Aspects of Yourself. The health of your body, mind, emotions, energy and alignment to source are directly related to the cosmic dimension you are in. The second step in this spiritual guide book is dedicated to this understanding.

In the lower dimensions there is little consciousness of health. Instead, there is a willingness towards self-harm. A person is not concerned with improving him or herself. Often they are lost in a mist of unhealthy behaviors that destroy the body and confuse the mind. Lower dimension people are not yet conscious of their energy body or Lightbody. As a result, they move in the direction of their pleasures, even when they harm themselves or their family members. There are often addictions that keep them circling in a pattern of confusion. Because they are not aware of their greatest good and because they are full of darkness, they just don't care and can become very unhealthy and sick.

During the growth dimensions, there is an awareness of health. In the 3rd and 4th dimensions, a person starts to heal themselves. A person has the intention of improving their body or disciplining their mind away from negative thinking. They may want to improve how they feel and work towards emotional healing. They start to become aware of early childhood trauma and how these events impact their current life story. If there is an addiction, they work hard to overcome it.

When a person first starts to grow in consciousness, the focus of healing is self-improvement. The motivation is egocentric. They may want a better body to attract a mate or to improve their career. They may want to discipline their mind because they want to attract abundance and have a positive outlook. They may be required to go to counseling to avoid losing a life partner who can't deal with their angry mood. As the five aspects heal, the person notices that they feel better and that life is good.

Toward the end of the 4th and into the 5th dimension, there is a shift in perception. Healing transforms from egocentric to spiritual practice. A consciousness arrives and the person begins to devote all physical practice and disciplining the mind to spiritual advancement. The body is viewed as the temple and the mind is viewed as an instrument of the soul.

A person becomes conscious about energies. There is an intuitive feeling about positive and negative energy in people, places and situations. A person becomes familiar with the subtle energy body and through the process of prayer, contemplation and meditation becomes aware of the soul. If there has been formal religious indoctrination, there is more consciousness about moral code. Healing the five aspects is dedicated to spiritual growth and purification.

In the 5th and 6th dimensions, the person feels like they have completed their healing work. They have made substantial progress and are ready to help others. Once you move beyond the 5th dimension toward the higher dimensions, it is assumed that you are healed. You have accomplished this step and can move forward in the progress of spiritual advancement.

The five aspects make up how you express yourself in the world. All five of these bodies are interrelated. If you improve any one of the five bodies, all aspects of yourself will improve. Imagine you decide to improve your physical body. You start exercising and change your diet. In time you've lost weight, improved your heart rate and started to feel good about yourself. Your physical body improves. Your overall holistic health improves which advances your cosmic dimension.

If one wants to advance in cosmic dimension, one can choose to focus on one aspect of oneself or one can work holistically. Some people will choose to focus on just one aspect of themselves. Other people will choose to focus on all aspects of themselves. Still others will ignore the whole process.

Everyone is moving at their own unique pace. You determine your intention for how you would like your life to go. The more you intend to reach optimal levels, the better you feel. You notice your life has an easier f low and you move in the direction of your life's purpose. The higher dimensional consciousness is attuned to love. The more centered you are, the greater the feeling of love. Likewise, the lower dimensions are centered in fear-based emotions. We can train our emotional body to attune to the positive emotions of love and become more neutral about fear-based emotions.

Seek to improve your physical body through diet and exercise. Seek to improve your mental body by eliminating negative thoughts. Learn to discipline the mind through meditation. Ask your emotional body not to overreact. Seek to feel positive emotions, such as love, light and joy. Energetically, find space that allows you to breathe, feel good and clear your chakra system.

Many imbalances occur because we are disconnected from our Lightbody. It's important to find ways to connect and seek a relationship with Divine Source. There is no right way to connect, there is just the right method for you at your level of understanding.

There are many ways to connect to Divine Source. Some people will choose to follow a religious path. Others prefer an individual path. You can connect to Divine Source through many activities. You just have to remember to devote the activity to spiritual pursuit. Many people connect through meditation, walking in nature, practicing yoga, eating healthy foods, dedicating their workouts to Divine Source or a number of other activities that can be spiritualized through intention. We need to feel connected to receive energy from Divine Source which animates us and gives us joy.

HEALING YOURSELF, HEALING OTHERS

Advancing in the Cosmic Dimensions means there is growth in spiritual consciousness. Many of us spend decades evolving in the 3rd and 4th dimensions. We are born into dysfunctional families. Some are deeply wounded and have to heal. Others get lost in early adulthood and have to redefine what is important to them. Some get lost in addictions along the way.

All of these narratives require finding ourselves and healing ourselves. As a human consciousness, we are moving into the 5th dimension. All will find their way through their journey in their own time.

Most of us are 3rd and 4th dimensional. We know we need to heal ourselves. We are aware of our shortcomings. We spend decades working diligently to heal our bodies, quiet our minds, calm our emotions, clear our auric fields and define our relationship with our infinite self. The fact that we start out with chaotic stories causes us to search. We spend time developing our skills and learning information in order to heal ourselves.

First, we heal ourselves and then we heal others. We move from needing help to knowing we can be helpful in the world. What started as an intention to exercise grows into a regular habit. What started as a 10-minute meditation evolves into a weekend silent retreat. What started as difficult yoga practice moves into yoga teacher training and leading others in practice.

> **We continue to evolve. All actions are spiritualized. All moments are mindful. All intentions are sincere. We become aware of our energy bodies. We communicate with our angels and Masters. We find ourselves healed or almost healed. We understand our life purpose. We are ready to be helpful in the world.**

Some of us are born with high dimensional consciousness. Many in the younger generations are advanced due to their evolution that took place in prior lifetimes. They hit the ground running. They know they have psychic gifts and find themselves in homes with loving supportive parents who nurture their higher consciousness. These young ones are the hope for our future. They are here to change the world.

Once we get to the 5th dimension, we are healed. Our spiritual practices are defined. We accelerate very quickly. We can transverse across multiple dimensions and commune with loving grace. Every day becomes a good day. We appreciate our life experience and we honor our mission. We become the healers and helpers we are meant to be. We start the noble effort of shifting everyone in the world from negativity to grace.

Chapter 4. Understanding the Role of Karma

WHAT IS KARMA?

Karma is the recorded history of wrong choices. If we take a step in the wrong direction, it means we have harmed ourselves or harmed another person. When we harm, there is the need to purify. A record is kept. Through the process of correcting wrong choices, our soul grows in the direction of the light.

There are two types of karma. The first type is your total score or tally over the course of a soul's journey. This is a soul's karmic tally. At the end of a lifetime, there is a review of the choices made throughout the experience. If we have harmed ourselves or others, this is taken into consideration in terms of additional growth that the soul still needs to learn. If a soul injures, steals, lies, cheats or sins, this is recorded. Karma is related to incorrect choices. Karma reflects those aspects of the soul that are impure.

The second type of karma is immediate karma. We have heard it expressed as, "What comes around, goes around." You take an action and the energy of that action returns. Immediate karma concludes its energy cycle in a short period of time or within that lifetime.

Immediate karma is energetic. It is the play of push and pull on experience. If we lie or take a shortcut, we move out of integrity. That lack of integrity leads to a negative outcome. Even if one lies and no one found out, there is an eventual return of that energy. It might be immediate or there may be a time delay. The resulting karma may be completely unrelated to the original mistake. The lie could result in attracting a negative consequence like receiving a parking ticket the next day.

When we incarnate, we are separated from Divine Source. There are both elements of light and dark on Gaia. Humans are granted free will and choice. We are allowed to create and enjoy an experience. But, there is a moral code. While we are journeying, we should not harm ourselves or harm others. And when we do, there must be a correction for our mistake. Karma is the tally of the record that is kept.

DIVINE SOURCE EXPERIENCING

Divine Source is a field of white light, the originator of all that is. Each individual's soul essence is birthed from Divine Source.

We separate and become individualized. Divine Source brings forth pieces from the whole to form individual cells. Both Divine Source and its cells are composed of the same light energy.

Divine Source is consciousness and energy. As a creative force, it seeks to grow and experience. In order to grow and expand, Divine Source creates experience. For experience to occur, two actualities need to happen. First, the whole must separate from itself to appear as other. This provides relationship and interaction. Second, there must be an opposition. This provides contrast to what one is not.

Divine Source created individual souls in order to have an experience. We are birthed from that essence. We are created from that energy. Divine Source is all consciousness. Each of Divine Source's cells are having an experience. Divine Source is also having all of those experiences through consciousness. Whatever we experience, good and bad, is recorded.

All experiences become part of Divine's Source's database of experience. As an individual cell, we are only conscious of our own unique experience. But from the perception of Divine Source, consciousness is having all experiences. Each cell is learning about love and its contracting shades of light. Divine Source experiences all these shades of light. All consciousness is being recorded. Thus, each independent experience adds to a database of Divine Source experiences.

We are on a journey to learn and grow. We are learning about love. We are becoming enlightened. We are individual cells contributing to consciousness. As we journey, we add to the inventory of experience. We are growing as separate individuals and simultaneously, we are growing as a whole unit of Divine Source consciousness.

THE PURPOSE OF KARMA

The purpose of karma is to learn about love.

If we are mean or selfish, we hurt someone. With immediate karma, that pain comes right back. This experience of pain asks us to question, "Why did I do that?" With immediate karma, we start to understand when we are standing in integrity or when we are not. The basic principle is that when we are in integrity, life rewards us with many blessings. When we are out of integrity, life is experienced with pain and suffering.

Total karma teaches one about love through long-term work. Many of us have made many poor choices that were not in alignment with love, when we have hurt others deeply. There is a justice system. Through the experience of repeating life lessons, one learns about love at a soulful level.

At the conclusion of one's life, there is a review. This is an inventory of right and wrong choices. If wrong choices cause harm to self or others, there is a need to redo the experience until the lessons are learned and understood.

Karma is the record of actions performed in darkness and ignorance. These acts need to be balanced and understood. This is the justice system. If one harms someone, the Law of Karma requires that one make amends. When we are separate from Divine Source and in the play of emotions, we can make wrong choices. All of this is understood and considered.

Divine Source is pure light energy. Inwardly, each cell yearns to return to the light. In the light there is no darkness. In the light there is no separation. Once we are separate, we have a certain amount of impurity. This impurity, if too strong, prevents us from returning to the light. In order to return to the light, we must purify ourselves and rid ourselves of karma.

KARMIC SCOREBOARD

Every time we are born onto the planet, we are made to have amnesia. We are unaware of our karmic score. One goal of the soul's journey is to reduce the karmic scoreboard to zero point. We want to erase all bad karmic points, to resolve all past wrongs. We receive a passing grade at the end of our journey if we have reduced the karmic scoreboard to zero point. If one comes to the end of their journey and still has impurities, the journey continues. One has too many impurities to enter into the light.

Primarily, we incarnate to experience. Secondarily, we incarnate to erase karmic debt. We undo a wrong action by performing its opposite. We can care for someone we have harmed in our past. We can give away something we value, like money or service. We can do good work. If we caused suffering, we can become a healer. If we are burning off a negative emotion like anger, we might manifest a disease. If we have been destructive, we may come back to rebuild. If we have created war, we may seek to create peace. If we have created a weapon, we may come back and create a tool for the greater good. If we have injured the earth, we may come back to repair it.

There is a certain script that governs our direction. We are governed by our internal desires and personality traits. We make decisions that affect the outcome of our reality. Within that program, there is freedom. We have choices to make.

Life is like an amusement ride. There is a governing track. But because of free will and choice, we can go off track. Oftentimes, the universe will assist us with a course correction. But we have the choice to ignore messages. We have the choice to not complete the ride.

As one moves through life, there are times when karma comes up. Events occur that seem random, but really they are based on our karma. We need to correct something in our unconscious past. We want to erase karmic points. We get a disease. We find ourselves in a bad situation. We lose our home in a natural disaster. Something happens that changes the course of our lives. These life events can be based on karma that needs to be cleared.

Life changing events occur because of our karmic scoreboard. The event was written into our script in order to help us clear karma. In the moment, the experience doesn't appear to be occurring for our overall good. But in the course of our soul journey, we are repairing an imperfection that will return us to purity.

Other times, uncomfortable events occur because of immediate karma. If one drinks alcohol, drives a vehicle and accidently kills oneself, this is an example of immediate karma. One made a wrong decision and it had a consequence.

People make wrong decisions. If we harm, we add more karmic points to the scoreboard. Sometimes another person will accidently become the victim of a wrong choice made by another. If a drunk driver harms another person, the victim's destiny has changed. Events have occurred based on another person's free will and choice to harm. This is unfortunate. The perpetrator receives karma for the harm they have caused.

Life, then, is a virtual reality. Just like a video game, when an avatar dies, it ends the game. Then we hit the restart button and it starts a new game. Whether we play the role of the perpetrator of the crime, or whether we play the role of the victim, both start a new game. The end game is reviewed and the new game is based on the underlying karmic score. This karma propels each of us forward into the next reality of experience.

ZERO POINT IS THE GOAL

After one becomes conscious of karma, one doesn't want to accumulate any more negative karma. The new goal is to work off karma and move in the direction of zero point. As you are mastering the steps of the cosmic dimensions, you are naturally avoiding karma, because you are moving in the direction of love and away from harming self and others.

If a mistake is made, karma will conclude its cycle immediately. There is an immediate correction. This immediate consequence prevents one from making further mistakes. A Light Worker would not harm, tell a lie or steal. One understands they will receive karma for these impure actions. There is no desire to experience karma and one follows a strict moral code. One has learned their lessons.

The primary teachings of love, compassion, forgiveness and acceptance become one's intention. Once conscious of karma and how it works, there is no interest in making incorrect choices. The focus of one's reality becomes loving oneself, loving others and doing no harm.

If you are 5th dimensional or higher, you are working on purification. Your focus becomes doing good work and becoming a healer or a helper. Service to humanity and spending time in spiritual practice reduces total karmic debt. Because the soul is carrying little karma, it is near zero point. Because the soul is doing good work, it is earning rewards and life currently, and in the future, just keeps getting better. Advanced souls have no karma and continue spiritual practice which serves to burn karma for others or the world.

Chapter 5. Resolving Karma

OUR CURRENT LIFE STORY ....

Earth is a working planet. It is not a vacation planet. If one has incarnated on Earth, one is here to grow. This is big work and it is challenging. Your reality is your curriculum. Your conscious dimension is your grade level. Your total karma determines your starting point. We are all working toward graduation to ascend into love.

Before one incarnates, one is presented with a script for how life might unfold. One is placed in a location as a character. We are each assigned life lessons, obstacles, rewards and purpose. One is placed in the right time for our lessons to be learned. What one does with the experience is a matter of choice.

One understands their life purpose. One has a general idea of what they want to accomplish, but the outcome is uncertain. When one is on their path and working on their purpose, they are motivated. One is focused and lives life in present moment consciousness. When one is not on their path, they feel stuck. One feels stalled out and knows intuitively they are not meeting their true potential.

One is assigned lessons to master. Lessons can be learned easily, or lessons can take lifetimes. Often, patterns repeat. Lessons teach us about ourselves. We question, "Why did I do that?" Or, "Why is this pattern repeating? What am I missing?" This self-reflection causes us to grow.

Life obstacles are written into every lifetime. Obstacles provide drama. One might rise to the occasion or fail miserably. One is forced to deal with certain situations. Obstacles are meant to be challenging. One develops determination. One's morals are tested. One has to make choices. Our ability to self-sacrifice is tested. One may choose courage, one may choose despair.

Obstacles demonstrate what one is trying to master. Obstacles present themselves in narratives through financial, relationship or health issues. All of us have obstacles to help us grow. There are many life lessons tied to obstacles. As we overcome an obstacle, we work towards mastery of a lesson.

If we were meant to have something, we would have it. If we don't have it and we desire it, then it becomes our goal. Money, for example, comes easily to some and not to others. Some people are born into money and are very unhappy. Some lose all they have worked for. Others come into money. Some have no money and are full of joy. All of these stories serve to teach us lessons about contentment, abundance, work ethic, sharing, exchange of energy and more.

Relationships provide interaction and drama. We need love. We look for a partner. Some people find each other easily and others struggle through relationship issues. Parenting a child teaches us about compassion, patience, our legacy and many other potentials. Relationships provide storyline. Some of us prefer quiet and independent lives, while others prefer a household of children. Each relationship presents its own unique demands. Keeping our physical vehicle healthy is a challenge area. Many are born with disease or develop one during their lifetime. Others struggle with not liking their body. Many are born with good health and allow it to decline. Lessons are learned through the body. When our vehicle is healthy, we feel good. When our vehicle is unhealthy, we suffer.

Within our story, there are also life rewards. Good things happen to good people. Rewards may return immediately. If one shares a smile, it will return. Rewards can return after longer periods of time. After a career, one is recognized for their joyful attitude. When one practices the attitude of love, they will create positive rewards and soften negative experience.

Rewards are also earned in the current life through hard work and integrity. Rewards are based in love. Abundance is a reward that comes from understanding one is part of all that is. There is enough for everyone. Rewards can also come from Divine Source and the Masters. We can receive a blessing when we ask with a sincere heart.

Rewards carry over to other lifetimes. There are points in our lives where doors open. Money comes in. A partner is found. A healer changes someone's life. Good work in any moment returns rewards.

Our current life story is real and yet unreal. It exists in linear time and yet it is virtual in the scope of infinite time. One is in the process of the story unfolding. This is the reality one is focused on. This is the reality one is conscious of. One agreed to play this character. We are the main characters of our stories. Our journey is full of challenges, obstacles, lessons and rewards. We move in the direction of our purpose. The best thing one can do is walk in love, light and joy.

KARMIC KNOTS

Sometimes we need to clear karma from past lives. If we have been in a relationship with another and it caused harm to both parties, there is karmic residue. Both people need to learn about love, compassion, forgiveness and acceptance in order for the karmic residue to be resolved.

....

A karmic knot is defined as a relationship experience one has to move through. One would prefer to walk away from the situation, but a karmic knot forces both to deal with the relationship.

....

Both life paths require them to stay working on the relationship. Both people are knotted to the experience. Both grow from the relationship.

It would be easy to walk away from certain situations. Karmic knots give one the opportunity to resolve past harm. As we work through the situation, we resolve disputes in this lifetime and in past lifetimes. Both resolve karma in the relationship. These relationships are carried over from past lifetimes.

One doesn't understand why they move through a difficult experience. One doesn't understand why they have to continue to be in a relationship with this person. This person presents as a challenge in their life. As one overcomes the challenges of the relationship, both grow and resolve karma.

Examples of karmic knots are found in these relationships: couples, parent-child, siblings and friends.

Couples have families. If they separate, a karmic knot develops. The parents may prefer to avoid the relationship. Child-rearing requires parents to deal with the relationship. A weak mother learns self-esteem. A controlling father deals with his anger. Both are forced to deal with power issues. There is an opportunity to grow in love and forgiveness.

A child is born to abusive parents. The child has no choice but to bear the abuse. The child will have to grow and heal from the situation. Both the parents and the child face repeating unhealthy patterns if they do not

heal from the situation. The parents must ask for forgiveness for the pain they have caused. The child must learn to forgive. Many lessons are learned in this karmic knot.

Sibling relationships are life-long. When we have issues with our siblings, we may choose to distance ourselves. However, a karmic knot might present if a parent gets sick and the siblings have to communicate. The situation requires interaction until the parent crosses over. The dispute might also carry over if there is an inheritance involved. This causes the siblings to work on relationship issues.

Friendships can develop a karmic knot. Two women have been friends for many years. They live in a small town in the same neighborhood. One friend betrays the other by having an affair with her husband. This is a karmic knot because they dwell in close proximity and live nearby. Both must learn from the experience.

These are a few examples of karmic knots. When a karmic knot presents, the best choice is to model love. The other party may not be able to return love, but what is important is that the one advancing in cosmic dimension expresses love.

RESOLVING CURRENT LIFE KARMA
THROUGH JESUS CHRIST

Masters from the Light Realms are guiding our path. There are Earth Masters and White Light Masters. Earth Masters have incarnated on Earth and we can reference their stories. Scripture has recorded their messages. They model for us how to live a loving life. White Light Masters dwell in the Light Realms. They are pure in their essence. They assist us to grow.

Masters advocate for our forgiveness and settle our karma. Before determining karma, a soul asks Divine Source for forgiveness. If the soul has not asked for forgiveness, a Master may advocate to Divine Source. If our sins are forgiven by Divine Source, the Masters determine the karmic scoreboard.

There are many Masters guiding us. Buddha, Krishna and Parmahansa Yogananda are examples of Earth Masters who guide us. These Masters cannot forgive our karma directly. They can go to Divine Source to request forgiveness on our behalf. Jesus can forgive karma directly. Jesus is a direct Son of God because he was in the first group of souls birthed from Divine Source. This first group of souls birthed by Divine Source are considered sons and daughters. Divine Source authorized Jesus to forgive karma on Earth.

When a person prays to Jesus to forgive karma, He erases all their karma for this current lifetime. This assumes one takes Jesus into their heart and works to purify themselves. While Jesus can forgive one for their wrong choices in this lifetime, he cannot erase one's entire karmic scoreboard. It is important that one asks for forgiveness and seeks to purify themselves. It is important that one feels worthy. The reality of human life is that it teaches us about love. The Light Realms understand that it's challenging and that mistakes will be made. Forgiveness is generously given.

FORGIVENESS & PURIFICATION

Higher dimensional consciousness requires one to practice forgiveness. One has to forgive themselves and others. The soul's journey is winding. All make mistakes. Pray for all karma to be cleared for wrong actions, known and unknown.

Ask for forgiveness from those you have harmed. Others hurt by our actions need to hear from us. Otherwise wrong actions are buried and become deep knots. One should take action to resolve karma during the current lifetime.

Send the one you harmed a card, or give them a call. If that person is out of your life, connect to them in prayer. From your Higherself to their Higherself, make a connection. Ask them sincerely to forgive you. Even if you don't know their response, know that the Masters have heard you.

The hardest part for most is forgiving oneself.

Review your life story. Say a prayer and ask for forgiveness. Put it all to rest. Forgiveness demonstrates how far one has grown. Forgiveness creates self-worth. Forgiveness heals the heart and sets one free. After forgiveness, there is purity.

Purification is an ongoing process. Purification is an act of devotion to Divine Source. It is a spiritual practice. Spiritual practice teaches one about oneself. As one practices, one observes one's thoughts, feelings and tensions.

Perform a purification ritual. Wash away karma with purified water. Water can come from the ocean, or a mountain river. Holy water can be found at a spiritual place.

Make a commitment to purify yourself through spiritual practice. Start your devotion and eventually it will become a daily practice. If you fall off the path, start back up again. Even if some days it feels like a chore, stay with the challenge. Be courageous. Spiritual practice is fulfilling. It refines and polishes the diamond inside.

WAYS TO RESOLVE KARMA

There are many ways to resolve karma. Stand in integrity with the light. Once you become conscious of how karma works, you would never want to perform actions that add to your karmic scoreboard.

One can do good work in one's vocation. Healers work in service to others. Vocations need to match your dimensional consciousness. In group settings, one can practice forgiveness during internal conflicts. One can listen and give empathy. One can smile and bring joy into a room. One can choose to not participate in gossip and complaining.

Give money to charity or someone in need. Acts of compassion resolve karma. One may decide to give time and service to others. Hold strong intentions about what you want to experience in your life. First focus on your needs, then pray for others and the world. Prayer directs angels to specific people and locations.

Find a spiritual practice and devote it to Divine Source. One can study scripture, meditate or go to church. One can draw angel cards or use mala beads to chant. One can practice an energy exercise. Tai Chi, Qi Gong and Yoga practice help increase the flow of prana in the body. One can spiritualize any exercise by dedicating each breath and body movement to Divine Source.

Perceive your physical body as your sacred temple. Treat it with care. Eat high dimensional foods and drink lots of water. Retreat into nature. Breathe fresh air. Create sacred spaces and spiritual rituals. Sing a joyful song, paint an inspired picture or write a book. When you create art, you are channeling divine energy.

Healers help people resolve karma. Pray to find a healer to assist you. Energy healers move prana through the chakras. This dissolves karma over time. If you keep experiencing anger, learn how to love. Notice negative patterns. Patterns repeat until lessons are learned. Once one masters a lesson, one moves forward.

Meditation and breath-work discipline your mind. Stop worrying and spinning negative thoughts. Learn how to expand the Lightbody into limitless space. Floating on waves of cosmic light reconnects one to the Light Realms.

Ordinary tasks can be devotional acts. Be mindful while driving or standing in line. Be joyful while washing the dishes and folding the laundry. Be devoted to your family and children. Perceive the child as the guru and offer love and care.

Most importantly live a joyful life. Change what you don't like about your life. If there is something you can't change, move into acceptance with it. Allow Divine Source to fill you with joy. Heal yourself and then heal the world.

Chapter 6. The Game of Karma

SPORTS ANALOGY

Incarnated souls, angels, Masters, Christ Consciousness and Divine Source all have different aspects. One way to understand is to use the metaphor of sports played on the field. Football, for example, has athletes, coaches and assistants, the league president and owners.

At the top of the football league are the owners. The owners control the stadiums, appoint the coaches and have a great love for the game. Divine Source is considered the owner of everything. Divine Source is observing creation and experiencing the game play. Divine Source owns both opposing teams and therefore always wins.

Divine Source experiences all the games at once. Divine Source knows all the strengths and weaknesses of the players. Divine Source wants all the players to win the trophy and advance to greatest. Divine Source hired all the coaches and is seeking an interesting Sunday afternoon, watching an equally matched game. Divine Source loves everyone and knows everything about the game. All is perceived as individual and all is perceived as one.

Divine Source appointed Jesus Christ as president of the league. A leader was needed to head the organization. A public figure could unite everyone. Jesus has top organizational duties. He leads the conference for the coaches. He greets and welcomes the players to the field. He gives second chances to the players. He loves, forgives and forgets. He sets the tone and vibration of the organization. He gives the trophy at the end.

Humans are considered the athletes on the field. The athletes run the plays and score the points. Athletes move the ball across the field. They want to win the game. In order to be successful, they must prepare for the game, work out and study plays.

Athletes get injured. An opponent can tackle and take them out of the game. Athletes make mistakes. If a play is forgotten, the athlete lets down himself, the team and the coaches. Players accidently fumble the ball. At times a player sits on the sidelines. An athlete can become demotivated and lose interest in the game.

Athletes have team spirit. Some will rise as leaders. Players bring their attitudes to the game. A player uplifts the team or brings it down. A player shows dedication to the sport. A player supports other team players. Players feel honor when they are victorious. A player can be a star athlete. An athlete has the opportunity to shine when one crosses the line.

Coaches are appointed by the owner. The Masters are considered the coaches for the athletes. They advise but don't run the ball. They create the plays but cannot score any points. The Masters can anticipate how the other team might respond to the action, but they have no control over how the other team plays. Coaches report to Jesus because he is the president of the league.

Coaches want to win the game. Coaches talk to the players and listen for feedback. Coaches hope the players will listen and be motivated. Coaches are involved in every play. They take responsibility for the players. Coaches live vicariously through their players. At the end of the game, they review the plays.

Angels are in a supportive role. They run all the errands and make sure everything is in place. Angels help the coaches and the athletes. They take direction from the coaches as to what duties to perform and when. Angels assist the coaches at practice. They make sure all the equipment is in good working order. Angels inform the coach if an athlete is in need of something.

Angels are assigned to specific athletes. They help the athletes with their workouts. They suggest a healthy diet. Some angels have general roles. They make sure players have food and water. They provide first aid. Some angels have specialty roles. They may advise a player on media presence or how to be a good role model. They are friendly and supportive. They always give words of encouragement and know exactly what to say.

Divine Source grants free will and choice. Divine Source has infinite time and space for the game to play. Divine Source hopes for an interesting game. Divine Source hopes for success for the athletes but is allowing of all outcomes. Masters and spirit guides are rooting for the human athletes on the field.

WHITE LIGHT MASTERS

Masters are elders in the Light Realms. There are millions of souls advanced to this state of reverence. Masters are benevolent. They are teachers, advisors and guides on our journey. They are compassionate and loving. They are fair and not harsh. They are experts in a field of study, similar to a professor. One can call on a Master to help guide their course in the world. If one is interested in learning a specific study, like yoga, acupuncture or energy healing, a specific Master might offer his guidance.

Jesus holds a higher rank. He was appointed by Divine Source as highest Master over Earth. Jesus serves on all councils. This is a difficult concept for the human mind to comprehend. There are divisions in responsibility. It is safe to think of having a team of support. Ultimately, all Masters are of Divine Source and emulate love.

The Masters are less emotional. Their consciousness is loving kindness. It is incorrect to think of them as angry with us or being disappointed if we make mistakes. Masters have our highest interest at heart. They completely understand the setup of the game of physicality.

They understand its purpose. They are not judgmental, but are tasked with resolving injustices and harm to self and others. The matters of karma and justice are complicated and deserve thoughtful review.

The Masters are assigned by Divine Source for the purpose of justice. Masters seek to be fair. Masters have thoughtful deliberations. They are individualized and have an astral form. They are representatives of Divine Source. They work in committees. They make suggestions and present different outcomes. They seek harmonious resolution. They do not always agree.

Many Masters have completed several soul journeys. They were born from Divine Source. Similar to cellular division, they became individualized and began to have experiences in physicality and in the astral realm. They evolved themselves to Master in the Light Realms. An elder Master could have completed 20 soul's journeys or more. The Master incarnates from time to time to present new teachings, give inspiration and insight.

FATE VERSUS DESTINY

Before we are born, we have in mind the goals we would like to achieve. Destiny is a potential of our story, but it is not written in stone.

One might be destined to be a musician, but if this person neglects to take a risk and audition, he may never play. How we choose to play a role is strictly up to the soul.

Fate is also written into the script. Fate is a prior arrangement made before we were born. This arrangement is necessary to provide some aspect that helps us to develop our story.

We need fate to assist us in our destiny. We are meant to meet certain people in our life who play vital roles in our development. We could not have done it without them.

While there is a general story line, it is a live creation. Anything could happen. Each of us has free will and choice, thus creating several possible outcomes. There are no guarantees. There are potentials. All is determined by our choices and the actions we take. Positive destiny is determined by our ability to focus on what we want and not be distracted from the path of our heart.

We may find ourselves in situations we did not intend. Fated life partners may get lost and fail. If one story line concludes without success, another story line will develop that allows for the same lessons to be explored. Eventually, we find our way to completing our life purpose and learning our life lessons.

We may fail or we may succeed. This is totally up to each unique person. In life sometimes people get lost. They make wrong decisions. They can't forgive themselves. They may develop an addiction or have a lifestyle that prevents them from accomplishing their goals. They fail miserably. And that's okay, too. This is also part of the play. Eventually one arrives in one's own time.

Lessons not learned are repeated. Of course, one never gets the same exact personality. One takes on a different character and tries again. Divine Source has infinite time and for that matter, so does each of Its cells. We have endless time to resolve karma. We have endless time to figure out what attitudes bring us joy and what attitudes dampen our joy.

Many of us are successful. We play our roles as we intended. We meet the goals of our life purpose and learn our lessons. We contemplate. We find our spiritual practice. We have a positive experience.

We feel, we think, we are alive in the personality of who we are. How fast we move through our lessons is completely an individual choice. All are granted the grace to move as quickly or as slowly as they intend. All are granted the grace to succeed or to fail. All are granted chances of different experiences to grow.

We grow in the direction of love. This temporary reality feels real as our vehicle is tied to emotional and physical responses. This experience is, therefore, real. We play many characters in the course of our soul's journey, but our personality in this moment will not exist for all time. Acknowledge who you are in this present reality. Be here now. Have no resistance and follow your bliss.

PROGRESSING IN SPIRITUAL CONSCIOUSNESS

As one grows in spiritual consciousness, one's life keeps getting better and better. One attunes to love and compassion. One prays for guidance and assistance comes. After you reach 5th dimensional consciousness, your life improves, and you find yourself moving in the direction of your life path.

Each lifetime provides the soul with lessons about love. The higher the consciousness, the greater the desire to share and heal others. A high spiritual consciousness assists one in waking up faster and remembering who they are. One arrives more capable of healing and helping.

Advanced souls come to loving families and are raised in spiritual surroundings. These souls are born with Masters inside their chakras and with spiritual gifts that present at a young age. Advanced souls are provided for in order to do their work. They have an understanding to go with the flow. They are born to parents who mentor them. Parents who nurture their children and encourage their gifts, speeding them along on their way.

Rewards for good works show up in positive events. Opportunities arrive to learn healing skills. Money arrives when it is needed. Prayer requests are answered. The right healer appears if the soul needs assistance. One finds themselves in service to others. Life is full of beautiful moments.

CLEAR KARMA, EARN REWARDS

Raising your spiritual dimension changes your life. Become conscious. Stop accumulating karma and start earning rewards. This awareness shifts one's life and all your future directions. Spiritual practice works off remaining karma. Good works earn rewards.

Ascend to your highest level of cosmic consciousness. Recognize your desires. Work to fulfill them. Understand that internal longings are clues to your life purpose. You are meant to fulfill those goals. Many want to be healers and helpers. Do service work. Serve others and serve the planet. Follow these yearnings. They will lead you to joy.

Recognize that worldly desires lower your consciousness. Worldly desires take one off the path. Worldly desires can keep you attached. Worldly desires are mental longings, like wanting to win the Olympics or desiring to be rich. They don't free you; they keep you in bondage. Purify yourself from dark qualities. Seek to rid yourself of negative habits and behaviors that you know are not good.

Ask to be in the company of the Masters and the angels. Ask that Light Beings come to your side. Engage in spiritual practice. Spiritualize your exercise. Bless the food you eat. Clearing your energy body and spending time in meditation raises your consciousness. Surround yourself with positive friends and environments. Feel the lightness of your being. Praise Divine Source. Ascend towards joy. Dedicate your activities to growing in the light. Be full of joy. Life is a beautiful gift. Attune to love. Feel glad to be alive. Explore the beautiful landscape. Appreciate what Divine Source has created. Imagine we are blessed to be on this journey. Be thankful for life abundant. Be full of love and let your light shine through.

Chapter 7. Negative Aspects of Karma

OVERCOMING CHILDHOOD TRAUMA

It's important to overcome childhood trauma. Karma, the purification of wrong actions, is one reason for childhood trauma. The other three reasons for childhood trauma are: challenge level, a predetermined plot twist, or a child who is a victim of another's free will and choice.

Before a soul is born, one understands the nature of its birth family. One cause of a horrible childhood is karmic momentum. In childhood, we often clear our karma. Children who are abused by their parents are experiencing karma from past lifetimes. Children born into traumatic situations like starvation, war or another event are the result of karma. Children who are born with disease are also experiencing karma and their parents' karma.

Childhood trauma can also be related to the challenge level. A soul might be born to God-loving parents, but find themselves in a location or circumstance that is difficult. The environment might be full of darkness. The family might be starving. A natural disaster may have occurred that causes the family to despair. Challenges will affect the child. The child's difficult experience serves as an obstacle to overcome.

Some childhood traumas are predetermined. They present as reasons for growth. An outside influence causes an uncomfortable situation. It was understood before one was born that a parent would die. The family decides to move to a different location causing one to lose a close friend. There might be an unexpected change in status. A wealthy child may suddenly lose its fortune. A sibling might be born who changes the family dynamic.

A child can also be a victim of another's free will and choice. They may have loving parents and enjoy their birth location and still suffer an experience at the hand of darkness. Sexual traumas often occur because someone is a victim rather than because of a past wrong action. The obstacle of the situation is unfortunate. The abuser will receive karma for their action. The child needs to seek healing to overcome the trauma.

Humans need to clear childhood hurts and pains. Our perceptions are shaped by our parents and the energies of the childhood experience. A person who has healed feels neutral about childhood trauma. A person knows one is healed when there is no emotion when speaking of the trauma. An adult moves through forgiveness and acceptance as they heal. They are no longer conflicted with false beliefs and negative patterns.

Injury in the early part of childhood will often give one a reason to seek healing and self- reflection. Being neutral means that one still remembers the experience, but there are no difficult trauma emotions to cause one to feel anger. If one notices triggering too hard and too often, there is a need to seek healing and release negative patterns learned in childhood.

One should try to identify false beliefs. For example, "I am not worthy" or "I am unlovable." One can reprogram oneself to think positively. Resolving childhood issues assists one to avoid repeating negative patterns. Childhood trauma helps one in deciding who they want to become. One remembers how their parents treated them and how it harmed their life. Conscious awareness teaches one how to treat their children. This can change the dynamic of the lineage.

Overcoming early childhood trauma is part of the process to help a soul remember who they are. The process of healing can guide them on a course towards being a healer for others.

THE ROLE OF THE VILLAIN

Souls will incarnate to play the role of the villain. All roles are governed by karma. No rules state that a soul must play the role of a villain. Some souls purify and remain in high consciousness. These souls grow in dimensional consciousness and do not receive roles as villains. The game of life on mixed-dimensional Earth is difficult. Souls do fail at points along the journey. Unpredictable twists and turns create a variance in outcome. Free will and choice determine directions on the path. Potential story lines are dynamic.

**Villains provide contrast to the light.
Hardships provide mountains to climb.**

Challenges to the light provide growth, learning and accomplishments. Without villains, there is no motivation for movement in the direction of the light.

All souls are assigned roles according to their karma. A series of wrong choices leads to a downward spiral. Wrong choices produce more wrong choices. The role of the bad person is appropriate for their development. Villains are born with negative tendencies. Dark energy is imbedded from their past karmic experiences. Humans in the lower dimensions have negative traits to overcome.

Anger and fear are found in dark environments. Vengeance can grow on Earth. Dark astral forces recruit souls with angry hearts. Villains have contracts for money and power. Some souls prefer the role of villain. Souls are attracted to the pleasures of the dark. A soul's wrong action accumulates karma. The downward spiral creates a negative cycle.

Some souls work with the dark. They perform their contracts. These souls are dangerous and harmful. These souls are far from grace in their journey. They are attracted to dark places. Their journeys continue in the lower dimensions, until such a time as there is a change in their hearts.

Some villains are weak souls. Souls are manipulated by the dark. Many have no intention of turning towards the light. Some souls die feeling unworthy. These souls neglected to ask for forgiveness. Shame keeps them down. Dark forces find lost souls and recruit them to cause mischief.

Earth is a mixed-dimensional realm. Divine Source allows the dark forces to incarnate as souls from the lower dimensions. Divine Source made rules. For every eight souls birthed from Divine Source, two are birthed from the dark. These souls perpetuate darkness in the world. The drama unfolds. Mixed-dimensional realms serve the purpose of providing souls choice. Villains play a necessary role in the game.

All souls who have lost their way are given opportunities to find themselves. For those in the middle dimensions, there is spiritual warfare. A tug of war between light and dark forces plays on the soul. Because the soul is not grounded in integrity, there is opportunity for moral decay. Often there are positive and negative voices, each encouraging the soul to take a different path.

Some souls get lost on their journey. Karma accumulates. A downward spiral can occur. There is darkness on the planet, but the angels and Divine Source never give up. The light within might awaken in the villain. A soul that prays will invoke a blessing. Although souls do get lost, many others overcome the dark.

COMMITTING SUICIDE

Committing suicide is a sin. Forfeiting one's own life creates self-harm and harm to others. Karmic consequences make matters worse. Every soul returns to council for reflection. The soul continues their physical experience.

The Masters are compassionate. The council is matter of fact. The council performs its duty. The life is reviewed.

The new life experiences are just as difficult as the last. The soul repeats the uncomfortable lesson. The goal is to experience life to the end.

Souls that commit suicide may become Earthbound. They are afraid of council and realize they have made a mistake. Angels appear, but the soul may choose to flee. This is dangerous for the soul as some will be deceived by the dark. Eventually, the soul returns to review its mistakes. The soul has delayed its process but still must continue its plight.

Some souls feel relief when the angels appear. The soul is tired and wants to rest. The soul is taken to the Waystation. This is an entry point before the Light Realms. Some souls are so tired they go dormant. They are allowed a period to rest. Then the angels awaken the soul. The soul is cleansed and made ready for council.

The Masters coach them. The soul is informed about harm to self. The Masters grant graces in the next lifetime. The soul may meet a healer. The soul may be rescued after a suicide attempt. Sometimes a child is predetermined to give love. Souls that commit suicide can get lost in the game of karma. A soul may be lost for a series of lifetimes.

Some souls are humanoid, and some souls are volunteers. Volunteers are those souls from a higher dimension. These souls agreed to participate during the Ascension. Some volunteers get lost. They are angry at Divine Source. They don't understand why they are in a dark place. Unconsciously, volunteers don't resonate with humans. They feel like they don't belong. They want off the planet. They have forgotten they are here to help. They have forgotten they volunteered to serve as Lightworkers.

These volunteers are disconnected from Divine Source. If they harm themselves, they receive karma.

These souls find themselves in difficult circumstances. Even though volunteers are hurt deep inside, they want to be healers. During the Ascension, their spiritual gifts will awaken. They feel conflicted. They no longer want to be on Earth and yet feel they have an important purpose.

Many volunteers receive blessings. As they awaken, they remember their vow to service. They start clearing karma. They awaken their spiritual gifts. They remember coming from a higher place to elevate the earth. Many volunteers pray, "Why am I here?" Those who call out will receive a blessing. They will move from lost to found. These volunteers will reconnect and serve humanity.

A person on earth with suicidal ideation has likely committed suicide in a past life. They must resist the urge to forfeit their life. Suicidal thoughts are signs that past lives need to be cleared. Healers assist others in overcoming thoughts of suicide. Healers can help those in need find their path. In the light, they will find their gifts. Lightworkers ascend to new heights. Now is the time.

PHYSICAL AILMENTS AND ACCUMULATED KARMA

Physical illness is related to karma. The physical body can reduce karma through manifesting an illness. The karmic scoreboard records wrong actions. Ascension to the Light Realms requires our score to reduce to zero point. Some souls choose to reduce karma through the physical body.

Before taking an incarnation, the karmic scoreboard is reviewed with the Masters. The soul's journey eventually ends. As souls approach the end line, the need to reduce karma becomes important. A soul and council might decide that a physical illness would assist the soul in reducing karma. Physical ailments work off karmic debt at an accelerated pace.

The illness decreases karma for many reasons. Karma creates negative energy. Negative energy must be burned like fuel to zero point. Souls can extinguish negative energy through asking for forgiveness and purifying themselves. These actions reduce karma. However, if a soul is unconscious, spiritual practice is not a focus. The soul has to reduce karma and negative energy another way. The physical body is allowed to express negative energy through a disease.

Organs in the body are aligned to negative emotions. The heart organ is connected to the heart chakra. If the heart chakra is overwhelmed with anger, the heart organ may resolve it through disease. The heart organ is allowed to express this residual anger. Once the negative energy is expressed, it is absolved. This is one example of how the physical body takes on unresolved issues. Hopefully, one releases negative emotions consciously.

Liver disease is an example of an organ resolving negative emotions. Some souls drink alcohol to numb negativity. Negative feelings are uncomfortable to hold. Negative emotions become energy blocks in the body. They can't express or heal. Fear and shame stay buried. The soul continues to numb the body. The toxic energy and poison in alcohol consume the liver.

Illness decreases karma because it creates narratives that inspire contemplation. Thoughtful discourse leads to forgiveness and acceptance. A soul might question, "What is life and its temporary nature? Why was I born this way? Why do I suffer?" It forces the soul and its family to examine esoteric questions. Contemplation assists the soul to search, leading to new understandings.

Many lessons are mastered through illness. The sick person must be courageous. They must surrender, trust and accept. They are presented with the opportunity to overcome a challenge or pass from the earth with grace. The soul can reflect on what caused this suffering.

The supporting family and friends readjust to serve the suffering soul. They are blessed with the opportunity to support and encourage. They are inspired to ask, "How can I help?" Karmic situations allow supporting souls to make amends for lifetimes when they hurt the soul with the disease.

There is an opportunity to practice forgiveness when souls experience loss. Cancer, for example, may bring a person and their family to contemplate death suddenly. The temporary nature of life is realized. Life is short. Most want to forgive and to feel forgiven. Illness provides an opportunity to clear past karma.

There is an opportunity to learn compassion, "I love you, no matter what." Children wounded by their parents come to aid in the dying process. Parents who have never known true love, learn compassion when a child becomes sick. Priorities of life are reorganized. The heart chakra opens. Hearts are mended. Negative energy is released.

Physical ailments inspire hope. All hope the soul that is sick will heal. The soul realizes how precious life is. The soul considers health, what they might have done differently, or what they might do in recovery. Some even hope for a miracle and are amazed when there is grace.

Souls pray when they are ill. Prayer connects us to Divine Source. One should communicate their intentions as a daily practice. But others are not conscious of praying until there is a trauma. Suffering inspires prayer. Trauma serves to cause everyone to ask for mercy. Mercy comes from a source bigger than their consciousness.

Illness inspires contemplation of, "Where do I come from and where do I go?" Souls contemplate after a loss. Moving through the dying process causes all to ponder. Those who have faith take greater leadership in sharing their wisdom. Those in ignorance are faced with deciding what they believe.

An advanced spiritual soul might contract a disease to burn off karma from past lives. An advanced spiritual soul might also contract a disease to burn off karma for humanity.

All of these considerations give souls an opportunity to reduce karma. Through the act of releasing negative emotions there is a reduction of karmic debt. Physical ailments cause contemplation. Through physical ailments many lessons are mastered.

PHYSICAL AILMENTS AND CHALLENGE

Physical imperfections are related to challenge level. Before a soul is born, the soul and council may decide for a more challenging lifetime. The higher the challenge level, the more opportunity to resolve karma. Dealing with an illness or handicap creates challenges. It is often predetermined that a soul will get an illness or have a handicap.

Strength comes forward when challenges are met. Disease and handicaps create narratives for mastering lessons. Supporting families make lifestyle changes that benefit all. Courage to overcome challenges provides opportunities for growth. Perseverance is required. The ability to complete tasks and work towards goals in spite of difficulties teaches determination.

The challenged soul needs to rely on people for support. The supporting family members become caretakers. Souls with purpose to be caretakers may fail the challenge. This situation resolves or creates karma. The challenged soul and its family must deal with grief and loss. The soul must learn to advocate for their needs. They need to accept offers of assistance. Handicaps teach a soul to surrender. Handicaps require people to overcome disabilities. Souls prove their power. A soul with a disability allows healers and helpers to serve. Silence replaces noise if one of the five senses is impaired. Not being able to hear or see cultivates silence.

Physical disease challenges lifestyle. One might develop a food allergy that requires the soul to purify its diet. This allows the family to understand how food affects the body. Some disabilities create friendships. Participation with peers with similar disabilities changes lifestyles. All benefit from sharing with others moving through similar lessons. Unique bonds are developed through mutual understanding.

When a soul becomes sick, they investigate how to heal themselves. One may search for a healer. The act of moving through the healing process may inspire a soul to become a healer. Hypnosis for emotional concerns allows the soul to experience trance states. This might start a meditation practice. Solutions to illness invite investigation of healing techniques. A soul might discover herbs, acupuncture, yoga practice, organic food and other methods that create a healthier life.

Some diseases and handicaps happen because others have free will and choose to make wrong decisions. Some corporations value making money over people's health. Wrong priorities have injured many. Toxins in the environment create disease. These diseases may not have been predetermined or karmic.

Some souls sacrifice themselves for others. Veterans believing in freedom can be injured. A person may give up a kidney to save another. A police officer may take a bullet protecting the community. Self-sacrifice creates honor and compassion. Rewards of valor are given for brave acts.

All of these situations give rise to resolving karma and mastering lessons. A person with a disease or handicap is meant to learn through these experiences. These experiences are caused by accumulated karma, current life karma, challenge levels, free will and choice and self-sacrifice.

Chapter 8. A Soul's Journey

A SOUL'S CONTRACT

When a soul decides to incarnate, it commits to live approximately 1200 lifetimes of experience. Each set of 1200 lifetimes completed is a soul's journey. The soul's journey concludes, and the soul is asked to consider five teachings from the experience. Is the soul purified enough to return to the light? Does the soul feel it has mastered its lessons? Is the soul's karma near zero point? Does the soul feel beautiful? Is the soul free from attachments?

The answers to these questions affect what choices the soul makes next. The light is at a high dimensional consciousness. The soul must be 5th dimensional or higher to merge. The soul and council consider the karmic record. A soul might feel ashamed if it has made too many mistakes. The soul considers if it has mastered the curriculum. The soul must radiate an inner beauty. Attachments to the world may keep the soul bound to physicality.

A soul separates from Divine Source and is born. This allows the soul to have an individual experience. In oneness, the soul experiences the light. As a human, the soul experiences light and dark. The soul must make a choice at the end of its journey.

If the soul is at 5th dimensional consciousness or higher, the soul has choices. The soul can choose to commit to another soul's journey. Many souls enjoy the adventures of physicality. Life is exciting. More experience will develop a soul. Souls continuing their physical experience serve the light. Souls have accumulated rewards and potential experiences will be positive.

A soul may want to enter the Light Realms. The Light Realms are vast. Light Beings engage their passions. The Light Realms are recreational. Light Beings play. They dance, sing and make music. They create art. They study a vast variety of subjects at universities. Studies include the Astrodome, galactic cultures, metaphysical arts, ancient histories and countless other subjects. Light Beings wander in the beautiful Light Realms. They spend time with their spiritual family. Leisure and relaxation are experienced.

Souls can ask to become angels. This choice requires them to transition to the Angelic Realms. The Angelic Realms are a different dimension where the angels dwell. Angels have a separate landscape. They have responsibilities and purpose. Many angels aspire to become Masters.

A soul can also ask to merge back into Divine Source. It is understood souls release their individual expression when they merge into oneness. All experiences are forgotten as they merge into Divine Source. Most souls prefer to retain their individuality.

A soul that is at 4th dimensional or lower, will be informed by the Masters that their journey will continue in physicality. As the soul starts a new journey, the karmic scoreboard resets to zero. Karma must still be released and understood. Rewards are carried over.

Many souls have completed several soul journeys. Twelve hundred lifetimes feel like a long time to our limited consciousness but, in the scope of infinity, it's all relative. A soul wants to experience situations to learn and grow.

Each time a soul commits to a soul journey, one runs the risk of getting lost in the game of karma. We are infinite. At times, we want to experience the Light Realms. Other times, we want to experience physicality. It is difficult in limited consciousness to conceive of never-ending time and space.

THE SOUL'S JOURNEY COUNCIL

Before a soul journeys into physicality, a large council of Masters is formed in support of the soul. This is the Soul's Journey Council. It consists of 1000 to 2000 Masters that will serve as advisors during the course of the 1200 lifetimes.

Some of the 1000 Masters will serve during several lifetimes. There are other Masters which are considered specialists that come in from time to time according to guidance needed in a specific field of study. If a soul were to become a medical doctor or healer for a tribe, a Master with that specialty background might serve on council for that lifetime.

At the end of the journey, the Masters know the soul very well. Each Master will submit a vote regarding graduation to the Light Realms. At the end of deliberation, it is Divine Source that decides. Divine Source strongly considers the votes of the overseeing Masters.

THE LIFETIME COUNCIL

Before each lifetime, the Lifetime Council gathers. This council has 20-50 Masters on their committee. These masters oversee the soul's lifetime. This council will deliberate on the karmic scoreboard at the conclusion of the life.

The Masters listen to prayers. They make decisions about potential changes in the narratives. Since life is always changing and unpredictable, Masters can alter plans and make adjustments. This is one reason why prayer is important.

A soul can ask a Master to be on their council. In-between lives, a soul may meet a Master and request the blessing of their guidance. A governing angel might ask a Master to be on a council. Divine Source might invite Masters to council. Masters are often invited because of a specific reason pertaining to the soul's intended purpose. All Masters that serve on the lifetime council also serve on the Soul Journey Council.

THE PRIMARY COUNCIL

A soul has a primary council. This is 10-12 Masters that serve on all 1200 lifetimes. These masters are with the soul the entire soul journey. The primary council is closest to the soul. As the soul advances in consciousness, these Masters play a direct role in teaching the soul sacred knowledge.

AFTER A SOUL TRANSITIONS

After a soul transitions, the Lightbody raises from the physical form. Four angels emerge to guide the soul back to the Light Realms. It's a three-day journey from the Earth to the Light Realms. Most souls know to follow the angels to the Light Realms. Some souls feel unworthy of love and choose to stay earthbound.

A soul might request a delay to say goodbye to loved ones. A soul might have unfinished business they want to take care of before they depart. An unexpected death may cause the soul to want to visit their loved ones. In this case, the angels agree to come back after a brief period of time.

Most souls follow the angels, especially those with a strong spiritual practice. These souls are excited to enter the Light Realms. The angels take them to an entry point. The soul is cleansed and purified. All dark energy comes off their Lightbody. There is an instant feeling of joy. Next, the angels take them to meet their loved ones already crossed over. They see their Masters and if they have followed Jesus, He will certainly be there. There is a great celebration.

Next, there is a time of rest and renewal before entering the Light Realms. Then, the soul reviews its life experience, first on its own and then with a few appointed Masters. It considers its journey with the lifetime council. There is discussion about learning their life lessons and fulfilling their life purpose. The session is therapeutic.

After council, the soul is invited to go into the Light Realms. They rest and enjoy themselves. Time passes, the soul is called back to council. The lifetime council of Masters has deliberated and made decisions about karma. This is made known to the soul. Then the soul is released back to the Light Realms. The soul enjoys the Light Realms in-between lives for 20 to 100 Earth years. During this time, the soul enjoys itself and waits for their dear ones to return to them so they can see them restored in the light.

DESIGNING THE NEXT LIFETIME

Before a soul reincarnates, the soul's lifetime council gathers. They evaluate what kind of journey the soul should embark upon. This is a collaborative discussion. There are five primary factors that determine how a soul chooses to incarnate.

The first thing that is considered is the life lessons the soul is in the process of mastering. A soul progresses through a curriculum of lessons. A soul is often working on mastering several life lessons at once. Sometimes it takes several lifetimes to master a lesson. Once a soul has mastered a lesson, it moves forward in the curriculum.

Along with the life lessons, a life purpose is written. These two items go hand-in-hand. A life purpose might be to teach, lead or inspire. A life lesson might be to learn about compassion, love or self-love. Lessons revolve around love, compassion, forgiveness and acceptance. Life purpose gives one a direction. A life purpose doesn't necessarily pertain to a vocation, although it can be the person's life work. A soul's life purpose might be to nurture. One life lesson might be to learn compassion. One could fulfill this purpose by being a mother. One could fulfill this purpose performing the vocation of being a nurse.

The second item that is considered is the karmic scoreboard. This is the scorecard of mistakes for which lessons must be learned. A record is kept of all harms done to self or others. The goal is to get to zero point and resolve all past harms.

The third item is unfinished business. If one was in the middle of resolving a karmic debt that was not completed, one goes back until it is resolved. A soul might have injured another and reincarnated with the purpose of caring for that soul. However, a natural disaster ended the life of one or the other, before the karmic debt could be completed. In that case, the unfinished business would be resolved later on in the soul's journey.

The fourth consideration is one's cosmic dimension at the time of transition, and the vibration of their energy body. These factor into family lineage, childhood trauma, health, spiritual orientation and wealth in the narrative. Higher consciousness continues in the next lifetime.

The fifth factor is challenge level. One can lead an easy, moderate or very challenging life. The challenge level is related to one's karmic debt. If one chooses a more challenging lifetime, it will be harder, but one will have more opportunity to clear karmic debt. If one has an easier lifetime, there is not as much growth work and therefore not the same level of challenge. If they have a high karmic debt to work through, many souls will opt for a more challenging life to see if they can resolve more karmic debt. Likewise, if they have less to resolve, they may choose an easier lifetime.

Reincarnation with a twin flame is discussed. Oftentimes a twin flame will request to share a lifespan with a soul. This, of course, depends on the life purpose of both souls and divine timing. A person's soul family is also considered. It is correct that one is often reborn into the same family. Some souls reincarnate together for a specific purpose. Soul groups are groupings of souls who work together on earth.

A soul knows a lifetime is going to be exciting or challenging. It is exciting to have a body through which to experience life. It's like riding a roller coaster. It's intense but fun, painful yet blessed. We move into free will and choice. We hope we will make the best possible decisions in the direction of the light. The more advanced of us hope strongly we will awaken from the dream.

THREE CHOICES

After recreational time in the Light Realms, a soul is called back to Council. Council has made decisions about reincarnation. A soul is given three to five choices of life narratives. The soul makes the final choice of their incarnation. The soul prepares to leave. The soul doesn't know exactly how it will go. One hopes it will accomplish its objectives. One says goodbye to loved ones in the Light Realms and departs for an experience in physicality. Before one is born, all one's memories are temporarily erased. The soul has to discover its goals and overcome its obstacles.

If a soul is spiritually advanced, the life purpose includes service to humanity and service to Divine Source. If a soul is still in mastery of life lessons, then its life purpose might be to master love, compassion, forgiveness and acceptance. If the soul has gotten stuck, it may need to repeat lessons, or continue lessons where it left off.

The soul starts its growth process where it left off. Each story will offer different obstacles and challenges. Each story has difficult events that will cause the soul to move through lessons. Sometimes, when bad events occur, it can be because of karma carried over from other lifetimes.

Each story has desires and aspirations that the soul can seek to achieve. Council helps to design the desires that the soul will be programmed with. That is why some people are born to climb mountains, others to succeed in business and others to practice specific talents like dance, music and the arts. These desires are predetermined and are meant to be achieved.

The soul decides on the landscape of the story. The soul considers what storyline will be of most service to the world, or will give them the greatest opportunity to grow. They consider if they want a public life or a quiet life. They decide if their family size will be big or small. The country, wealth and spiritual path are factors in the decision.

The soul considers the family lineage in terms of DNA, intellect, physical body and emotional development. The soul considers if it would like to be male or female. And finally, it considers if it would like to have children and how many. The soul doesn't choose its parents, but it is told by Council to choose from a selection of potential parents.

There are potential outcomes regarding soul mates and twin flames. A soul mate is defined as an intimate relationship that teaches one another about life lessons. A twin flame is a soul mate that shares a life purpose. A twin flame is a long term and significant partner. A soul can have many soul mates of both genders. Soul mates can be sexual relationships or friendship based. The attraction will be strong so both souls feel the need to be in the relationship. Potential twin flames are discussed. All of these relationships are discussed as potentials, not destined ones. More than one potential is available because others have free will and choice.

After these considerations are made, the soul makes a choice and prepares to incarnate. The soul goes to a different location in the Light Realms where it waits for divine timing to begin its journey. The soul is excited and aware of the challenge. The soul is aware it will forget its origins and disconnect from the Light Realms. This occurs so the journey will feel real. The soul hopes it will awaken and remember who it really is.

THE DELIBERATION OF KARMA

The Masters have thoughtful discussion in their deliberation of karma. Their ultimate purpose is to adjust the karmic scoreboard. They consider growth in the direction of the light, what life lessons were learned and what life lessons have yet to be understood. There are karmic consequences. If one murdered someone, there is justice. A consequence for that action is ordered and will be experienced later on during the soul's journey.

Considerations include unforeseen events not predetermined that occurred as the result of another person's free will and choice. Council considers intentional wrongdoing that caused harm to self and others. They consider less significant choices which showed a lack of integrity.

Missed opportunities are considered, either by their own doing or as a result of circumstances. Acts of self-sacrifice, where the person considered others before themselves, are honored. The purification of worldly desires and vices are scored. The purification of their body, mind and emotional reactions are scored.

Good works are considered. Time spent in devotion, spiritual practice and charitable actions are appreciated. Acts of heroism and honor are cause for high praise. Souls who served others are thanked for their good work.

The soul participates in the deliberations. One has a chance to review one's life narrative. Strengths and weaknesses are reviewed. Each soul gives feedback on accomplishments.

Most souls enjoy the process and feel the love and support of the Masters. All understand that one is experiencing in order to grow.

Chapter 9. Advancing in Spiritual Dimensions

THE ADVANCING LIGHTWORKER

Humanity is moving into the 5th dimension. Love and compassion are realized. The 5 Aspects of a person are healed. A person can ascend into the higher dimensions. Once a soul enters the 5th dimension or higher, they are considered a Light Worker. Spiritual gifts awaken for the Light Worker. These gifts bring insight and healing. These gifts brighten a dark world.

Some souls are born advanced in the higher dimensions. In past lives, they performed spiritual work and cleared their karma. Lightworkers are here to serve humanity. They are blessed with spiritual gifts. Others are moving upwards in dimension. Meditation is clearing their karma and connecting them to Divine Source. The Cosmic Ray, an energy that comes from Divine Source, is expanding. This energy is pushing human consciousness forward.

Humans forget who they are until they awake. A few children are awakened from birth. Some awake in adolescence. Others move through life stories before the flash of awareness comes. Upon closing one's eyes in meditation, a new reality dawns. The non-physical dimensions are reached. The Light Realms are realized as their third eye opens.

The astral dimensions exist within our physical dimension. Some Lightworkers sense light and dark energy that cannot be seen with the physical eyes. Internal whispers of intuition develop into conversations with angels and Masters. Many close their eyes and see colors, visions, or symbols. Some can see auras or dark shadows in the night.

The Lightworkers feel confused as this seeing and sensing is not understood by religion and modern society. And yet they know it is true through their own experience. The time is now to embrace, accept and respond to this invitation to ascend into the higher cosmic dimensions.

LOVING GAIA AND HUMANITY

Entrance into the 6th dimension or higher brings the consciousness that we are one. Lightworkers bring light to a dark world. All religions are one religion. All religions have a singular message: love yourself, love others, love the earth and love Divine Source. One creates their own unique path aligned to Divine Source. All serve humanity in its unique forms.

Lightworkers love Gaia. Gaia has a spiritual essence. She is mother and is conscious of all human activity. She is aware of human limitations. Lightworkers are sensitive to Gaia and want to help heal the earth. Unenlightened humans are destroying the earth. Lightworkers seek to do their part to balance the damage.

Lightworkers understand we are all one. The meaning of the word Namaste is realized. The light within honors and recognizes the light within all. The Light Worker is able to view everyone with love and appreciation. Even those lost in the lower dimensions are loved. Lightworkers understand they are here to serve humanity. Their work can be on a personal scale or with a large audience. The purpose is to inspire light, one touch at a time.

Lightworkers connect directly to Divine Source. They develop several techniques to reach up, connect and receive. This connection replenishes them. Most find meditation as their vehicle to hollow out and fill with love. Others have developed prayer, contemplation or other spiritual exercises that keep them whole. They are full and ready to serve in their purpose.

Lightworkers collaborate with Masters. Lightworkers move in the direction of their purpose. As the journey begins, Masters communicate through intuitions. Synchronicities open doors to life purpose. As their consciousness grows, relationships develop. Lightworkers attune to teachings coming from the Light Realms.

Human consciousness is ascending. The Light Worker is aware they play a role in this evolution. The first task is to awaken from limited consciousness. The next task is to assist others to awaken. The more people who are awake, the more light beams onto Gaia. The teachings of Christ Consciousness reach the multitudes.

The Lightworkers understand the principles of Christ Consciousness. They have internalized these concepts and model them for others. Each Light Worker finds a unique expression. Some will find an Earth Master and share their message. Others will tune in directly to the Light Realm. They share their wisdom as it comes.

Gaia will be made anew. Divine Source holds a contract with the dark. The dark is aware of its limited time on Earth as the contract expires. Gaia will transform. The question remains how many humans will ascend. How will Gaia be affected by lower dimensional humans?

Time is short. The Masters hope all will ascend. The dark is a worthy adversary. The question of the play and human ascension lies in the hands of the Lightworkers. Lightworkers change the dynamic of the play on Earth.

Lightworkers are aware of the delusion. They are wide awake and understand the manipulations of the dark world. Mass Consciousness will rise based on the forward momentum of Lightworkers. Eventually, the light will win. Divine Source is the creator of the Astrodome. Divine Source created the dark as well as the light.

Who will awaken and in what time frame? The dark will try to take souls and harm cities until it is removed from Gaia. The effort of the Lightworkers to awaken humans will create a smoother transition.

Lightworkers affect change through healing, teaching and spreading the light. Money is also a powerful tool. Lightworkers can make or break corporations that serve a profit-based world. Lightworkers should support businesses of higher consciousness. Lightworkers should withdraw funds from corporations that pollute and harm. Lightworkers can support businesses that promote health and healing. They can withdraw funds from corporations that provide unhealthy foods and lifestyles. Monetary support is a powerful energetic source of change.

Lightworkers are from higher dimensions. Volunteers are visiting Earth for a brief time. We are here on purpose to serve the light. Divine Source calls Lightworkers to action. All is well. One wakes up, connects to the light and shines brightly.

LIGHT REALMS AND THE ANGELS

Lightworkers are aware of the astral play. Astral, energetic and angelic are words that describe this realm. The astral forces are as real as the physical dimension. Lightworkers following their path begin to perceive the spiritual realms. Earth is involved in a play of light and dark. Humans have free will and choice. Humans move through their realities without awareness of the forces at play. Lightworkers become conscious of the unseen forces that interact and influence our world.

Lightworkers are aware of their angelic teams. Angels work together with Lightworkers. Many Lightworkers perceive angels, auric fields or other indications of energetic presence. Lightworkers communicate with their angels and Masters. This allows them to give healing and readings. This allows them to lead meditations and service the world.

A strong relationship between Lightworkers and angels develops. Lightworkers need angels to assist them with healing. Angels can clear dark energy from people and places. Lightworkers need the angels to protect them and move them forward on their path.

Lightworkers begin to feel protected. Spiritual confidence grows. They start engaging and interacting with their angelic team. They understand that calling in the angels helps their day to move more smoothly. They hear more positive thoughts. They receive guidance and perform their healing work.

Missions become clear as Lightworkers advance. Lightworkers ask to learn new spiritual skills. Masters start to take residence in the chakras of the spiritual student. Angels and Masters become available to guide, instruct and teach the Light Worker. They advance towards their spiritual goals. This person works in collaboration with their angels and Masters.

Angels are assigned to assist with everyday tasks. They provide healing voices and soothing energy. Angels comfort, protect and assist with the manifestation of prayer requests. Angels help you find the right person at the right time in the right location. They create synchronicity to provide that new job, friend or opportunity. They may rescue a person in a dangerous situation. They may provide intuition about how to cook a healthy meal or assist someone in the present moment.

Masters are guides and highly specialized in certain topics. A master might be assigned to assist one in learning about energy healing, crystals, divination tools, or esoteric topics. Masters guide the course of your life. They understand your intentions and what you are trying to accomplish. Masters come forward to lead the spiritual aspirant in the direction of their spiritual goals.

Lightworkers can perceive the astral realm in the physical dimension. Many Lightworkers report seeing ghosts or dark shadows. They can perceive lost souls or dark astral energy. They may advance to a point where dark astral energy might want to interfere with their work. These Lightworkers start to develop skills to combat attacks from dark astral energy. As their perception grows, they can fend off attacks and assist others to move out dark energies.

Lightworkers have a direct connection with Divine Source. They can explain the teachings of the Masters and that their purpose is to share what they know. They can see and communicate about the Light Realms. Lightworkers understand that all divine personalities are aspects of Divine Source.

SPIRITUAL GIFTS AND PSYCHIC POWERS

Spiritual gifts and psychic powers awaken for the advanced Lightworkers. The purpose of these gifts is to serve humanity. Some Lightworkers can channel messages from the angels and Masters. This allows them to give readings and help others find their way. This allows them to gain direct guidance when needed. It allows the Masters to communicate messages about healing the earth.

Not all psychics are aligned with Divine Source. Dark energy can grant psychic powers too. Spiritual bypassing refers to a person who develops psychic powers without being aligned to Divine Source. Lightworkers should align to Divine Source and hold the highest intention to serve humanity. Lightworkers have integrity and a spiritual practice. When they are spiritually attuned, they avoid spiritual bypassing.

Clairvoyance is the ability to see images, visions and symbols. These visions represent meaning and clarify direction. Clairaudience is the ability to hear voices from the Light Realms. Clairsentience is the ability to feel or sense energy that is not visible to the physical eyes. This allows one to see and explore the astral dimensions. Psychic experiences develop and become real.

Many Lightworkers become energy healers. They can purify themselves and become channels of Divine Light. They can help to direct divine light energy through others. They can direct healing rays of light into the chakras and expel negative energies. As they develop, they are able to move deep-seated karmic residue energy out of the higher chakras. This allows clients to heal at an accelerated pace.

Lightworkers understand how energy works. Lightworkers avoid dark energy in low dimensional people and locations. They can transmute dark energy into the light. These people radiate an energy field of white light. They bring in positive energy when entering a room. These persons' auric fields can brighten a room. Some Lightworkers may feel or see auras. Lightworkers that read auras help others to understand the energy body.

Advanced spiritual skills develop. A Light Worker notices they are telepathic with friends and family. Some become mediums and communicate with souls on the other side. Some provide counseling for those in grief. Lightworkers may assist lost souls in crossing over to the other side.

Other advanced skills include telekinesis. This is the ability to move objects with the mind or dematerialize a physical object and rematerialize it in a different form. Telekinesis also allows an object to dematerialize and rematerialize in a different location. Many Lightworkers have prophetic dreams. They will know things in advance of them occurring. This skill helps one to know what may occur and how to protect oneself. At first these skills may feel random and insignificant, but they are indicators of gifts that will develop over time.

Psychic skills assist Lightworkers to bring light to people and the world. They work with their angels and Masters to develop these skills. Lightworkers direct angels to certain places on the globe to assist in working against the dark. They can generate a funnel of Divine energy and distribute it outward to the world. All are here to raise the dimensional consciousness of the planet.

Lightworkers feel called to develop their psychic gifts. Lightworkers will feel called to learn energy healing. Lightworkers become aware they are telepathic.

TRANCE, HYPNOSIS AND PAST LIVES

Lightworkers practice meditation. Meditation teaches the physical body and mind to rest. The mind is calmed through focusing on the breath. The emotional body feels for love and joy. The energy body, which consists of the auric field and 100 chakras, begins to clear. The Lightbody, or soul, begins to expand. The physical body goes quiet. It fills with Divine Source. An altered state of consciousness is reached.

Lightworkers activate their energy body in meditation. The root chakra reaches down to anchor. The heart chakra opens to love and joy. The crown chakra reaches up and receives from Divine Source. Lightworkers call in their angels to clear energy blocks in their divine line. Lightworkers attune to Christ Consciousness. Oneness is felt. When attuned, one receives visions, information and directions about their purpose.

Meditation is a trance state. Meditation explores non-physical dimensions. Imagination is considered by modern science to be unreal. Lightworkers understand that imagination opens portals to other dimensions.

....

Imagination is an opening to places in the cosmos. The Light Realms are non-physical and hold no density. This doesn't make it unreal. This makes it non-physical.

....

Hypnosis is a deep trance. Lightworkers lead others into a deep state of relaxation. Hypnosis is effective for healing psychological problems. The person in trance is open to suggestions. Positive affirmations can reprogram the mind. Negative thinking can be deleted and replaced with positive affirmations.

Hypnosis allows for past-life regression. Lightworkers guide clients to inner memories of past experience. Clairvoyance skills are activated. Remembering past lives broadens reality beyond this current lifetime. Recalling these memories feels real as narratives and emotions come forward. Remembering past-life trauma removes irrational fears and habits. Relationship issues come to light. A person may experience a narrative giving them insight to present life experience. Some clients experience life on other planets. Some clients experience their life in other forms.

During hypnosis, clients can experience the Light Realms. The Natural Realm is a beautiful place. People can experience their inner sanctuary. Clients experience gardens, beaches, mountains and open spaces. Angels and Masters appear to give gifts and blessings. Clients can receive messages about their life purpose.

During hypnosis, clients can contact their Higherself. The Higherself is that aspect of a person that resides in Divine Source. The Higherself understands one's life purpose and why we are experiencing difficult circumstances. The Higherself can tell one what life lessons we

are seeking to master and what life changes would serve us. Divine Source can send energy to heal the physical body. Lightworkers will feel called to lead people in meditation. Lightworkers will feel called to learn hypnosis and take people into trance states.

MULTI-DIMENSIONALITY AND DREAMTIME

Advanced Lightworkers reach altered states without a guide. They travel to other dimensions on their own. They become multi-dimensional. Lightworkers astral travel, remote view or channel. They see other worlds that are beyond this one. They communicate with angels, Masters and galactics. They access these realms eyes open or eyes closed. The Earth plane is one of many realities that exist. Lightworkers cross over to other dimensions.

Lightworkers can open the Akashic Records. These records hold past lives on Earth and other planets. They are found in the Light Realms. Lightworkers gain access to the records. Information on life lessons is granted for themselves and their clients.

Lightworkers utilize healing tools that create meditation states and release negative energy. Meditation with crystals or meditation in natural spaces produces trance states. Rhythmical drumming and ceremonial dance create trance. The Light Worker will utilize many healing tools to create multi-dimensional spaces.

Lightworkers understand the benefit of sound healing, vibrating a bowl or using tuning forks. High vibrational sounds and theta waves create frequencies that expel dark energies and draw in light energies. These vibrations produce a sensation of floating.

Dreamtime is a state of consciousness. The Lightbody has the ability to explore the Light Realms as the physical body rests. The Lightworkers need to hold an intention to separate in dreamtime and explore different dimensions.

Astral travel is another word that describes this experience. Our Lightbody lifts out of our physical body and has experiences. If we request to visit the Masters during dreamtime, our soulful bodies will go to work with the Masters. Lightworkers learn about psychic gifts and receive information to assist on Earth. Lightworkers with galactic origins and Earth missions visit their home worlds or interact with galactics during dreamtime.

This is different than dreaming. While the physical body is at rest, our mental body creates dreams. The mental body is different than the Lightbody. Our mental body needs activity to process our physical experience. Our mental body puts together image fragments and creates dreams. Dreams have elements, fears, challenges and meaning pertaining to Earth stories. Dreams are random mental fragments. Dreams are also messages from the Masters to the conscious mind. Past lives are also remembered through dreaming.

Lower dimensional humans, and those unconscious of dreamtime, go dormant while sleeping. Lightworkers need to intend to explore the Light Realms. Lightworkers know upon awaking to ask telepathically what happened. Through channeling, they can remember where they went, what they experienced and what they learned.

The conscious mind upon awakening may not remember, but our Higherself has gained knowledge. Lightworkers access that information through connecting to their Higherself. Knowledge is triggered when a Light Worker goes to see a healer, reads a book or participates in a workshop. Lightworkers are intuitively familiar with the information.

Doors open to non-physical realms as Lightworkers progress. These realms are interesting and exciting. Lightworkers open adventures beyond the ordinary physical dimension. This physical realm becomes the virtual one. Lightworkers become aware that this temporary existence is not as real as once believed.

Lightworkers are connected to Divine Source. Lightworkers are allied with the light against the dark. Lightworkers heal humans of negative and fear-based energies. Lightworkers heal the Earth. Lightworkers prefer high dimensional people, places and situations. Lightworkers avoid lower dimensional environments. Lightworkers eat pure foods and appreciate natural beauty. They keep their divine line clear in order to feel love. Being of service gives purpose and joy.

The Light Worker shines brightly. Lightworkers serve as healers and helpers. Lightworkers journey as Earth Angels.

Chapter 10. The Volunteers

HUMANS WITH GALACTIC ORIGINS

Souls on Earth feel they resonate with galactic beings. Many humans are curious about off-world beings. Some humans believe they have galactic origins. They are conscious of their relationship to Pleiadian, Orion, Sirian or other galactic races.

Human comprehension of galactic origins varies. About 25% of humans with galactic origins are conscious they have spent time in other higher-frequency worlds. Another 25% are becoming conscious and will wake up over the next 50 years. Many have the opportunity to become conscious in this lifetime. Others will wake up during their next lifetime.

Having galactic origins means that you have incarnated in other realms besides Earth. Of the seven billion humans on Earth, about 50% are entirely humanoid. Their journey of experience was meant to be lived only on Earth. Another 25% have galactic origins and started incarnating on Gaia about 600 lifetimes ago. About 20% of galactics have lived on Earth for approximately 250 lifetimes. The final 5% are new arrivals who have been on Earth fewer than 10 lifetimes.

Most galactics have incarnated on two other higher-frequency planets, before arriving on Gaia. A fraction has spent time on five other high-frequency realms.

There are also many human hybrids. This means that their human DNA has been combined with off-world DNA. Over the millennia, many species have visited Earth and have produced interbred races. These hybrids are also considered galactics. even if most of their incarnations have been primarily on Earth. As a result of having different DNA strains, they have slightly different characteristics in terms of intuition, emotional response, psychic ability and spiritual awareness.

THE ORIGINS OF EARTH

Gaia's natural and biological species evolved over eons of time. Gaia was considered perfect. A physical manifestation of the Light Realms. Evolution produced dinosaurs. A comet destroyed their habitat. Eons after the dinosaurs left the planet, Divine Source created the Earth anew.

Humans were unlike animals. Humans did not evolve from apes. Humans came directly from Divine Source.

Humans are Light Beings from the Light Realms. As Light Beings all exist in Divine Source consciousness, there is no darkness.

Divine Source wanted Light Beings to comprehend the light. In oneness, there was no separation, no choice. Divine Source decided Gaia would transition to a free will and choice zone. Humans would experience life in physicality. They would create their reality based on choice. Divine Source allowed darkness to come to Earth. Divine Source granted darkness to persuade humans away from the light.

The dark challenged humans. Challenge creates growth and experience. The strong competitive ambition of the dark was given by Divine Source. The darkness needed to feel powerful or it would not be a worthy adversary. Darkness had an appetite to grow and conquer.

The dark created chaos in humans. Divine Source hoped humans would choose purity over darkness. Each individual soul would decide. Humans could live as they wanted. Humans could experience both light and dark realities.

Divine Source hoped souls incarnating as humans would return to the light. Through experience, humans would realize the consequences of living in darkness. The discipline of karma began. For every action causing hurt, another would arise to teach about the impure decision. Humans would experience how they treated others. Gaia allowed for this dramatic play to unfold.

ASTRAL VERSUS GALACTIC

All physical beings have matter or density. All physical beings are considered galactics. Humans are one type of galactic species. Galactics hold physical space in the Astrodome. The Astrodome means the measurable physical universe that humans are aware of. Divine Source created all of this; space, planets, stars and countless galaxies in our Astrodome.

The astral dimension is another layer that exists simultaneously within the physical realm. The astral dimension is described as light, energetic and etheric. It is translucent and holds no physical form. Our energy body and our Lightbody are astral and exist as a double imprint within and around our physical body.

The Earth's dimension also has an astral landscape that exists simultaneously. The astral dimension is unseen by our physical eyes, therefore it is unrealized by most humans. Energy healers and humans with psychic skills can feel, sense and see the energy body and the energy landscape.

Imagine glasses that allowed humans to see the astral landscape. This would change one's perspective considerably because one could see which people and environments were full of light and which were full of darker colors.

There is a distinction between astral and physical dimensions. The two dimensions interact with each other. Dark astral beings are allied with dark galactics and light astral beings are allied with light galactics.

Earth is a mixed-dimensional reality containing both light and dark astral energies. Light astral energies, which we call angels, interact with humans. Dark astral energies do the same. Astral beings, both light and dark, effect humans in physicality.

The Light Realms contain only light and the dark realms contain only darkness. The play of these two forces occur in physicality. The play of light and dark forces is strong on the Earth.

The Light Realms exist in a dimension beyond the Astrodome. The Light Realms are astral, energetic and translucent. This is where the Angels, Masters and Divine Source originate from. Angels are assigned to the Earth plane and operate within the astral landscape of Earth. Dark astral energy is also assigned to the Earth.

There are places in the Astrodome where only light dwells. These planets have a high dimension and most of the galactics are connected to Divine Source. To the contrary, there are no places in the Astrodome where there is complete darkness. Lower-dimensional planets have dark realities, but even then, light forces are working to raise the dimension.

DIVINE SOURCE'S GRAND EXPERIMENT

Three hundred millennia ago, Divine Source asked Gaia if she would participate in a grand experiment. Earth had been in existence for billions of years. Over this time, she had evolved and supported various types of life.

Divine Source decided to create a mixed-dimension planet and allow its inhabitants to have free will and choice. This meant that Divine Source would allow darkness to descend. Divine Source asked Gaia for permission to allow this experiment. She agreed, but it was also decided that after 300 millennia, she would be allowed to evolve to the next level of consciousness. What was started and agreed to also had a pre-determined end time.

Like all complex games, rather than there being a winner and a loser, the game was based on how long it would take to complete. Earth was to be the first mixed-dimension planet in the history of the Astrodome. Other planets in the Astrodome went through growth cycles, but the inhabitants were of similar design and dimensional consciousness. Divine Source decided to allow this grand experiment to observe the result.

The human drama of light and dark has continued all this time. Many souls at different points in their soul journeys have sojourned to Earth for the wild ride. Divine Source allowed the influence of darkness, while at the same time provided representatives of the light.

It is a struggle for humanoids. The cycle of karma became ongoing for most of the inhabitants. At several points in Earth's history, the darkness was strong enough to warrant a cataclysm that meant starting over again. Each time this happened, humans had to rebuild their society. A disconnection from Divine Source eventually resulted in chaos.

Darkness was strong and demonstrated its power. Visiting galactics from other places in the Astrodome also manipulated the purity of Divine Source's design. Humans forgot how to connect to the higher dimensions. Divine Source allowed the play to continue and chose not to intervene. Divine Source was curious to see how far it would go and how long it would take for humans to awaken. Meanwhile, the discipline of karma continued, and humans went on exploring its possibilities of light and dark.

Planet Earth became a popular destination for many galactics. Our planet is a bit of an anomaly – on one hand, beautiful, and on the other hand, dark. Earth was viewed as a free zone where galactics could experience without rules.

Divine Source had promised Gaia an end to the game. She also had her own path of ascension and it was always Divine Source's plan to allow her to move to her next evolutionary step. We have come to a place in linear time where we are 200-300 years from this end game. When this happens, Earth will be restored anew and darkness will leave Gaia. There is a contract in place.

THE HISTORY OF GAIA

For 300 millennia Gaia has served as a brilliant landscape for eons of story. Earth is unique in that the free will and choice zone has allowed battles on both sides to be won and lost. There is a free will and choice contract that governs our Solar System. Therefore, many galactics have been observing, interacting and interbreeding with humans on Earth.

Earth is a container for a mixed-dimensional experience. About 30% of all planets in the Astrodome are considered mixed-dimensional with both light and dark astral elements influencing reality. Gaia is unique and beautiful. She is one of most beautiful and diverse planets in the Astrodome. Her range in dimensional consciousness is wide, -1 to 30 dimensions. Spiritual understanding among the Earth population is broad. This makes Earth unique.

About 55% of planets are of higher frequencies. According to the cosmic scale described in the guidebook, 25% exist in 5th to 10th dimensional consciousness. Another 25% exist in 10th to 20th dimensional consciousness. Another 5% of planets range even higher, up to the 20th dimension. That means most galactics are practicing love and compassion.

Likewise, there are dark planets. 10% of planets exist in 3rd to 5th dimensional consciousness. The remaining 5% are hellish realms. These planets exist in -1 through 3rd dimensions.

There are over 4000 planets teaming with life in the Astrodome. Here is the overview: 30% are mixed dimensional, 55% are high dimensional and 15% are low dimensional.

Earth is about to graduate in dimensional consciousness. No longer will Gaia exist as a mixed-dimensional planet. She will transition to a planet that exists in 5th to 30th dimensional consciousness. That means all humans living in -1 to 4th dimension will no longer be able to reincarnate on Earth.

Gaia has already shifted to the 5th dimension. This change in dimension started in 2009 and completed its cycle in 2012. Now all species she supports must also make the shift into 5th dimensional consciousness to stay in experience in this realm.

Humans started shifting in 1960. Many of us awoke and started to question the limitations of our reality. The shift accelerated in 1992. After that, human consciousness continued to shift during acceleration points. 2012 and 2015 saw the most important peaks thus far. More are scheduled to follow to assist humans in finding their way.

Humans have 200 to 300 years to realize 5th dimensional consciousness or higher. That's about three or four more lifetimes and then decisions will have to be made. Lower dimensional humans will not be allowed to stay on Earth. Earth will transform to a light planet.

WHY OFF-WORLD GALACTICS ARE INTERESTED IN EARTH

Over the course of time, many galactics have interacted with Earth. Some galactics have visited to study humans and research the ecosystem. Dark galactics have also come to Earth. Influenced by lower primal instincts, they have come for reasons of conquest or to take resources back to their home worlds.

White light galactics existing at higher dimensions have sought to influence humans. Some galactics have presented themselves as Divine Sources. These galactics understood their advanced technologies would amaze humans. Many galactics had positive intentions. They wanted to help humans and didn't view their intentions as harmful. Still other, more advanced, humans are subterranean. These galactics have evolved in Earth's underground. The subterranean galactics are 5th to 9th dimensional. They, too, have presented themselves as Divine Sources and influence surface humans in positive directions.

Over millennia, astral forces have influenced humans. Angels and Masters have come to Earth to assist humans to find their way back to the Light Realms. Dark astral forces have also plagued humanity. They have manipulated, and created war and confusion.

> **All of these players — humans, galactics, light astral beings and dark astral beings — have intermingled on our planet, creating a variety of experience, creation and play. Like all good dramas, we are coming to a crescendo. Galactics observing humanoids ascending in consciousness is a rare event. It has only happened a few times in the history of the Astrodome.**

These players have a vested interest. Astral forces battle for souls. Those existing in the middle grounds of the 2nd, 3rd and 4th dimensions have an opportunity to ascend. Galactics have sent representatives to incarnate as humans to be of service to the light. These humans are considered the Volunteers. The galactics are assisting their Volunteers with guidance and protection. Meanwhile, dark galactics complicate factors. They are allied with the dark astral forces and represent an unknown in the evolving story line.

WHY GALACTIC VOLUNTEERS STARTED INCARNATING ON EARTH

A call went out from the Light Realms. Higher-dimensional galactics were informed that humans needed assistance in the Ascension. Souls were invited to incarnate on Gaia. Within a human vehicle, these Volunteers could make an impact. Humans can score points on the field. They can make a difference. Volunteers could influence the dynamic of consciousness.

The transitional period would take about 5000 years. Humans would start to move through a growth cycle. After a dark age, Masters would come to show the way. An acceleration in consciousness would slowly occur. Towards the conclusion of the cycle, the acceleration would exponentially grow.

The volunteers were called in to assist in the evolutionary process. The primary planets that volunteered representatives were the Pleiadians, the Orions and the Sirians. Other planetary systems also sent representatives. Some souls were recruited directly from the Light Realms. This would be a difficult assignment. Many souls volunteered to leave their comfortable high-frequency dimensions in service to the Divine Source. Volunteers were fully aware of the challenges of the journey. They would have to follow the rules of Earth and forget who they were.

Once they started on the path of human experience, they were subject to karma. There was the possibility they could get lost. If they made a wrong choice, they would be placed in their next life accordingly. They would completely forget their heritage and where they had come from.

There would be conflicts, as the range of dimensions would spread from -1 upwards through 10, creating a wide pool of variance in the population. Earth would contain hellish environments as well as safe havens. All would be mixing together, creating complications and the possibility of descending in dimension.

The Volunteers incarnated on Earth with no memory of their assignment. If they were successful, they would assist in the process of raising the dimensional consciousness of Gaia. But if they got lost, they could collect karma and suffer as a result. This was a dangerous assignment, because even though they came from higher consciousness, they could unintentionally descend.

At their soul's essence, they knew Divine Source consciousness.

> **Volunteers were higher dimensional. They would be part of the human race and yet feel separate. They would be inclined to participate in higher-dimensional activities of channeling, meditation and natural healing.**

Hopefully they would resist lower primal urges.

For lifetimes, they would have no clue as to their origin. Volunteers would move through the Earth experience. Earth's environments were abrasive compared to what they were familiar with. They were adjusting to fear-based energies and negative experiences. They were also exploring spiritual practice and religious paths.

Adjustment to lower dimensions would continue for several lifetimes. Volunteers were told they would remember near the end of the journey. They would wake up inside of the dream and realize who they were and why they came to Earth. Their mission would activate. They would know to raise the dimensions of Earth.

It is time for those Volunteers to awaken. That process is happening now. Volunteers with galactic origins are waking up to their background. Human consciousness has evolved, realizations can occur. Human dimensional consciousness didn't allow this 100 years ago. Now, Volunteers are able to discover their origins.

THE MISSION OF THE VOLUNTEERS

The change in dimensional consciousness is significant. It is time for humans to graduate to the next level. Countless souls deserve to move to the next level of experience. Divine Source knew humans needed assistance to ascend. The call went out to the higher-dimension planets requesting Volunteers come and lend a hand.

The mission of the Volunteers is to help humans ascend to the 5th dimension. Volunteers are transplants. They intuitively resonate at a higher dimension of understanding. Even those who have gone off course still have an internal knowingness that they didn't come from here. Volunteers are here to help and to heal the planet. They are further along in their comprehension of energy, spiritual practice and non-physical realities. They are attuned to the higher dimensions. Volunteers are less manipulated by television, money and earthly pleasures.

The Volunteers understand meditation, natural healing and organic farming. They are alternative thinkers and have non-conventional ideas. Some are awake to their galactic origins. They stretch their imaginations beyond the status quo. They desire to connect with Divine Source. They can see limitations and manipulations of historical systems.

This is an important job. Volunteers are here as helpers and healers. They seek to improve the corruption of corporations and government systems. They are pushing the human experience forward and waking up souls stuck in the 3rd and 4th dimensions.

Volunteers have never been alone. They are supported by their galactic brothers and sisters. They are watching from afar. The white light galactics provide protection. They are watching from the wings. They intervene during dreamtime. The galactics assist the Volunteers. They are helping them to awaken. Now is the time.

Part 2. The Spiritual Guidebook to Ascension

An Introduction

AN ACCELERATION IN HUMAN SPIRITUAL CONSCIOUSNESS

Most humans were only aware of the physical dimensions until the 1960s, when there were changes in consciousness. In the 1980s, the changes in human consciousness accelerated. Humans were open-minded to spirituality and multi-dimensional consciousness. Humans were able to perceive other realities through meditation, hypnosis and forms of trance. Plant medicine has also inspired a whole new set of spiritual enthusiasts that have journeyed into other realms and come back with great wonder.

December 12, 2012 marked the beginning point when more humans were able to start perceiving these non-physical realities. For example, on December 12, 2012 (12/12/12) about 8% of the population moved into the 5th dimension. Meanwhile, about 50% of the human race moved into the 4th dimension.

Humans at the 4th dimension were ready to consider ideas of multi-dimensionality. They created their own paths outside organized religion. Humans discovered past-life regression through hypnosis. Humans were introduced to ancient alien theories. Paranormal investigations were conducted. Humans reached out to galactics in meditation. Humans started to become more psychic and intuitive in general.

Now, in 2016, we are past the starting line. September 27, 2015 marked the date of the blood moon eclipse. About 15% of the world's population is 5th dimensional and about 56% has moved into the 4th dimension. The human race will shift higher until all humans reach the 5th dimension of Christ Consciousness. This will occur over the next 200 to 300 years.

Meanwhile, there is a schism in consciousness. Loving spiritual people are moving up in dimensional consciousness. Fear-based humans operating at lower dimensions are becoming more negative and desperate. Many lower-frequency people are presenting with acute mental illness. That is one reason why we are seeing more gun violence and war zones in hot spots on the planet. These people live in fear, anger and hatred. Humans in the 2nd and 3rd dimension have time to grow and make a different choice.

Gaia, the Earth, has also shifted her consciousness. She moved into the 5th dimension on 12/12/12. Therefore, all humans have to move to match her vibrational resonance if they want to stay on the planet.

Lower-frequency humans will not be allowed to reincarnate on Earth after this time. They will continue with their soul journey but will move to other locations that are a closer match to their lower frequencies. During the transition, the people of the earth will have a mixed understanding of spirituality.

HOW TO USE THE SPIRITUAL GUIDEBOOK

The Spiritual Guidebook to Ascension outlines 10 Cosmic Dimensions. A spiritual dimension is a frame of reference to help one assess where they are in their spiritual development. The 10 Cosmic Dimensions are further organized into 11 Steps, or areas of growth. One grows in the Ascension process moving step by step.

The Spiritual Guidebook can be read straight through, but it can be difficult to understand that way. The book was written like a math table: there is an x axis, "the dimensions" and a y axis, "by step". It is written vertically and horizontally. You can read it by dimension, or you can read it by step. In order to get the most out of the material, move through Worksheets 1–4. This helps you evaluate your current overall spiritual dimension. It also assists you to move through the material step by step. Once you understand your starting point, you can review forward or backward which allows you to see the progression of spiritual development step by step.

For example, if you determine you are 4th dimensional, then read through that section and make sure you agree. To advance in dimensional consciousness, look at the next section, 4th moving to the 5th dimension. Compare step by step. You will notice the subtle shifts in perception that place one into the higher dimensional consciousness. Likewise, you can review one dimension back, and see the progress you have made.

....

Once you start to consider the material, you may notice that in some steps you feel you are very High Frequency and in other steps you feel you are in the Growth Dimension. This is perfectly normal as we are all growing in different areas. The purpose of the work is to help you evaluate your spiritual progress and provide a roadmap for growth.

....

There are no rules, the Spiritual Guidebook is meant to be a flexible tool, and help you gauge your spiritual progress and set goals for growth. This spiritual guidebook is designed to help you consider concepts in spirituality. It can be helpful to show your strengths and weaknesses with the aim of improving yourself to your highest potential.

You can also assess the dimensional consciousness of a friend, family member, or client. This can help you understand if there are differences in spiritual compatibility. It can also help the spiritual healers understand what goals to work on with clients when they first come in for healing.

The 4th and 5th dimensions are presented in two phases. This helps one understand the progression of spiritual evolution. These phases are long and can take years to complete. Movement through these dimensions depends on how spiritually motivated you are to grow in the ascension process. It is normal for a person to spend many years growing and learning as they transform from the 4th to the 5th to the 6th dimension.

Once you are in the 4th dimension, you have started your spiritual search. Once you get to the 5th dimension, you are considered healed and working on your higher purpose according to your individual life plan. When you enter the 6th dimension, your spiritual gifts start to open. Beyond the 10th dimension you are now a spiritual teacher or an advanced healer.

Worksheet Material

The best way to go through the Spiritual Guidebook is to follow the worksheets on the following pages. The worksheets will guide you through the material and help you understand how it can be used as a reference for your own spiritual growth.

Worksheets 1 through 4 help you evaluate your current overall spiritual dimension, and move through the material step by step. These worksheets help explain how the material is organized and how you can use it as a self-reference tool for spiritual growth.

Worksheet 1
overviews your "overall" cosmic dimension

This is an identification marker that helps you determine where you think you are overall on the 10 Cosmic Dimensional scale.

Worksheet 2
organizes the 10 Cosmic Dimensions into 4 categories

This helps you to place your dimensional grouping. This is helpful as you explore the Spiritual Guidebook. You may choose to focus on dimensions in your category, rather than reviewing all the dimensions from beginning to end.

Worksheet 3
overviews the 11 steps

The 10 Cosmic Dimensions are organized into 11 Steps. As you move through the material, you may find that you rank very highly in some steps, but lower in other steps. This worksheet will give you an idea of where to focus to improve your overall dimensional score.

Worksheet 4
is a blank worksheet designed to assist you in working through the Spiritual Guidebook step by step

This helps you set goals to advance in spiritual consciousness. Use the Step by Step Worksheet for deeper self-reflections as you move through the first 3 steps that capture your interest the most.

Worksheet 5
focuses on Step 1.

The starting point on the journey is to love yourself. Many people are working in the area of self-love, self-worth, self-esteem and self-acceptance. This worksheet assesses more specifically the dimension you are working on in Step 1.

Worksheet 6
is on the topic of forgiveness.

Many people are working on forgiveness issues. This worksheet helps you to place your dimension for Step 1. You can evaluate forgiveness issues and self-reflect on deepening the love and compassion of the heart.

Worksheet 7
looks at Step 2.

This step reviews the 5 Aspects of the Self. It helps you determine your strongest aspect.

Worksheet 8
is focused on identifying relationships with individuals that are toxic and low frequency.

As you grow in dimensional consciousness, you might not be able to hang out with their negative energy.

Worksheet 9
considers where you are in the journey toward ascension.

You may feel that you need to focus on your spiritual practice to develop further. Many of you are ready to develop psychic skills or move in the direction of becoming a spiritual teacher or counselor.

Worksheet 10
is a self-reflection tool to help you consider the material.

The questions are organized first by dimensional groupings and then by the 11 steps. Considering these thoughtful questions moves you into Higher Frequencies on your journey.

Worksheet 1. Evaluation Your Cosmic Dimension

Below is outline of 10 Cosmic Dimensions. The Cosmic Dimensions measure human spiritual evolution and conscious awareness of spiritual principles.

As you read the overview of the 10 Cosmic Dimensions, STAR the dimension that most relates to you. Go with your first impression. Read over the outline below and get a general idea about where you fall on the scale.

AN OVERVIEW OF COSMIC DIMENSIONS -1 TO 10

-1   Dimension – Darkness Harm to Others
   1   This person is dark to others.
   2   They are malicious.
   3   They are mean-spirited, and harm themselves.
   4   They hate others and are destructive.

0   Dimension – Darkness Harm to Self
   1   This person is in dark and doesn't take care of themselves.
   2   They perform acts of self-harm, such as addiction, cutting themselves or developing eating disorders.
   3   They can be lazy or live off of others.

1st   Dimension – Darkness Unaware of Light
   1   This person is in darkness and has not done self-reflection.
   2   They are unware of the light and don't take care of themselves or their responsibilities.
   3   The may have a weak moral code.

2nd   Dimension – Indifferent to Light
   1   This person believes in God but doesn't feel connected.
   2   They are indifferent to the light.
   3   They satisfy their personal desires.
   4   They may or may not have a strong moral code.
   5   They don't believe in a higher power. (atheist)
   6   They don't know or haven't considered spirituality (agnostic).

3rd Dimension – Limited Perceptions of Light

1. This person has a limited perception about God.
2. Their perception of God is simplistic.
3. They have not experienced God directly.
4. They are religious but not open-minded to other truths.
5. They go to church on holidays, but don't have a spiritual practice.

4th Dimension – Journey to Light

1. This person is open to spirituality.
2. This person is a beginner on the spiritual path.
3. They are open to personal growth and meditation.
4. They listen to new ideas before dismissing them.
5. Many start therapy or find a healer.
6. This person had a plant medicine experience that has made them question God.
7. A connection to Divine Source has occurred and now they want to deepen it.

4th Moving to the 5th Dimension – Doorways to Light

1. This person is activity working on their healing process.
2. This person is investigating or has found a spiritual path.
3. There is new awareness and self-insight
4. They are learning yoga, meditation or another healing art.
5. They feel connected to Divine Source.
6. Their actions are loving and compassionate.

5th Dimension – Light Realms Christ Consciousness

1. This person is full of Christ Consciousness.
2. They feel clear and are moving forward.
3. They have found a spiritual path.
4. They are expanding in love.
5. They recognize oneness in everyone.
6. Their spiritual gifts awaken.
7. They feel healed.

5th Moving to the 6th Dimension – Light Realms Light Worker

1. This person is advancing on their path(s).
2. This person is learning a healing technique.
3. This person wants to serve the world.
4. Their intuition is strong.

6th Dimension – Light Realms Awareness

1. This person begins to develop psychic skills.
2. They are open to multi-dimensional concepts.
3. They are interested in divination tools.

7th Dimension – Light Realms Light of the Angels

1. Spiritual gifts and psychic skills are opening.
2. They want to become healers and spiritual teachers.
3. This person services the light.
4. They are further along in their spiritual practice and growth.
5. They bridge to the astral dimensions.
6. They may start to become aware of the galactic realms.
7. They focus primarily on spiritual concerns.
8. They are interested in energy healing or leading hypnosis.

8th Dimension – Light Realms I Am That

1. Their spiritual gifts and psychic powers are expanding.
2. This person is advancing on their spiritual path.

9th Dimension – Light Realms Oneness

1. This person is a spiritual teacher of teachers.
2. They are spiritual leaders within their communities.
3. They may participate in the astral realms and galactic realms.
4. They have a multitude of spiritual gifts.

10th Dimension – Doorways to Divine Source

1. This person feels Divine Source profoundly.
2. They hear, sense or communicate with their angels and Masters directly.
3. Their spiritual gifts and psychic powers are known to them and they are working towards mastery.
4. They are master healer in the world.

My Overall Cosmic Dimension is: _____

Go to the guidebook and scan that dimension you have chosen. As you overview that dimension in the guidebook see if you resonate with the bullet points. Afterward come back here and continue to Worksheet 2..

Worksheet 2. Identify Your Dimensional Grouping

The Cosmic Dimensions are divided into four different levels of spiritual evolution: The Lower Frequency Dimensions, The Growth Dimensions, The Ascension Dimensions and the Higher Frequency Dimensions. Which grouping do you fall into?

Lower Frequency Dimensions -1, 0, 1, 2

1. Low-frequency dimensions, -1, 0, 1 and 2, describe people who are not yet developed spiritually. They are malicious or full of self-hate, many are lost and confused.

Growth Dimensions 3, 4

1. The 3rd and 4th dimensions are considered growth dimensions. People are growing and learning in the direction of spiritual enlightenment. In the 3rd Dimension, people have an understanding of spirituality, but it is limited.

2. When people come into the 4th dimension, they are more open-minded about spiritual concepts and put more energy into walking the spiritual journey. They start to take workshops and develop a spiritual practice. They learn how to meditate and investigate spiritual topics and healing modalities.

The Ascension Dimensions 5, 6

1. The 5th and 6th dimensions represent Ascension. When one comes into the 5th dimension, they are healed and they feel good. They have arrived at a certain point in their spiritual development where they are healthy, practicing a specific spiritual path, and feel like they are ready to assist others in their spiritual journey.

2. When you move into the 6th dimension, you start to awaken your psychic skills. You start to receive angel signs and you know you are being guided down a certain path. You become aware of astral elements and can feel energies. You are drawn to meditation and sound bowls. You know you are further along on your path.

The Higher Frequency Dimensions 7, 8, 9, 10

1. The 7th to 10th dimensions are the higher-frequency dimensions. These people are further along in their spiritual path and spiritual practice. They are shamans, life coaches, ministers, or everyday people that are there to assist you or give you a sign.

2. Those people in the higher frequencies are interested in metaphysical concepts and developing their spiritual gifts. They explore concepts such as dreamtime, astral travel, past lives and the understanding that we are not alone in the universe.

The Grouping I Fall Into is _____

Understanding your dimensional grouping will help you to identify the steps you want to focus on. Let's review the 11 Steps next.

Worksheet 3. The 11 Steps – Topics for Consideration

AN OUTLINE OF THE 11 STEPS – TOPICS FOR SPIRITUAL GROWTH

The 10 Cosmic Dimensions are organized into 11 Steps. Each step represents a theme of spiritual development for the person. Briefly review Steps 1 through 11.

Step 1   Love, Compassion, Forgiveness, Acceptance

Step 2   The Five Aspects of the Self (physical, mental, emotional, energetic, spiritual)

Step 3   Relationship to Family and Community

Step 4   Spiritual Practice and Spiritual Attitude

Step 5   Relationship to Divine Source

Step 6   Healing Oneself and Healing Others

Step 7   Relationship to Humanity and Earth

Step 8   Comprehension of the Astral Realms and the Angels

Step 9   Awakening of Spiritual Gifts and Psychic Powers

Step 10   Comprehension of the Multi-dimensions

Step 11   Comprehension of the Galactics

Worksheet 3. The 11 Steps – Topics for Consideration

Each Cosmic Dimension is broken down by steps to help you evaluate different areas of growth in the Ascension process. Each step has questions and consideration for spiritual growth. Those that are newer on the spiritual path may find they want to focus on the Steps 1 through 6. The first three steps relate to yourself, your relationship with family and community and forgiveness issues. Below is an outline of the first Steps.

Step 1   Love, Compassion, Forgiveness, Acceptance
- **A)**   Self-Love
- **B)**   Self-Acceptance

Step 2   The Five Aspects of the Self
- **A)**   Physical
- **B)**   Mental
- **C)**   Emotional
- **D)**   Energetic
- **E)**   Spiritual

Step 3   Relationship to Family and Community
- **A)**   Forgiveness of Family and Community
- **B)**   Compassion for Family and Community
- **C)**   Expressions of Love, Joy, Peace

The next three steps focus on helping one to gauge their spiritual practice and relationship with the Divine. One moves into spiritual study or learning the healing arts. One becomes very interested in healing themselves and ultimately starting to heal others. Below is an outline for the next three steps.

Step 4   Spiritual Practice and Spiritual Attitude
- **A)**   Spiritual Practice
- **B)**   Forgiveness
- **C)**   Moral Code
- **D)**   Meditation

Step 5   Relationship to Divine Source
- **A)**   Relationship with Divine Source
- **B)**   Communication with Divine Source

Step 6   Healing Oneself and Healing Others
- **A)**   Healing Oneself
- **B)**   Healing Arts
- **C)**   Healing Others

Those that are further along on their path are working on psychic development and their service mission. Advanced spiritualists will be more interested in Steps 7 to 11. These steps discuss 5th dimensional topics and perceiving astral elements like working with your angels, psychic skills and perceiving the energy body.

Step 7   Relationship to Humanity and the Earth
     A)   Service to Humanity
     B)   Healing the Earth

Step 8   Comprehension of the Light Realms and the Angels
     A)   Communication with Angels, Signs and Synchronicities

Step 9   Spiritual Gifts and Psychic Powers
     A)   Intuition, Empathy, Manifesting and Synchronicities
     B)   Clairvoyance, Clairaudience, Clairsentience, Seeing or Feeling Auras
     C)   Channeling and Mediumship - Automatic Writing, Channeling
     D)   Prophetic Dreams, Precognition, Telekinesis, Astral Travel

Step 10   Comprehension of Multi-Dimensions
     A)   Trance, Hypnosis, Past-Life Regression
     B)   Energy Body, Lightbody, Dream Time, Present Moment Consciousness

The final step has to do with galactic awareness. If the galactic information doesn't resonate with you, let it go. Many people reading this work will resonate with these concepts. Many Higher Frequency people consider themselves "starseeds". People who believe they are starseeds feel they have incarnated from a higher frequency planet to assist humans and the Earth with the Ascension process.

Step 11   Comprehension of the Galactics
     A)   Ancient Alien History, Investigation of UFOs
     B)   Communication with Galactics

Worksheet 3. The 11 Steps – Topic for Consideration

Self-Reflection on Step 1

1. Based on the outline of the 11 Steps, which section seems most important for me to start?

    a) The first three steps, because I'm investigating spiritual growth and know I am working on myself.
    b) Step 4 through 6, I feel good about myself, I am developing my spiritual practice.
    c) Step 7 through 10, I am interested in expanding my consciousness, and service work.
    d) Several steps are interesting for me to evaluate.

2. Based on your interest, choose a Step 1-11 that you most want to consider. Write down the first 3 steps you want to consider.

    Step # _____

    Step # _____

    Step # _____

3. As you move through the Spiritual Guidebook, you will find it more helpful to read the guidebook step by step. Let's move through an example. Let's Review 3rd Dimension, the 4th Dimension and 4th Dimensions moving to the 5th Dimensions look just at Step 1 - Love, Compassion, Forgiveness and Acceptance. This will show us how the Dimensions change as you progress spiritually.

3rd Dimension, Step 1 – Love, Compassion, Forgiveness, Acceptance

1. This person begins to affirm, "I love myself and I deserve the very best." They are moving in the direction of self-love.

2. This person desires to develop love and compassion towards themselves and others.

3. This person begins to move in the direction of understanding compassion.

4. This person moves into the light and asks forgiveness for their sins.

5. This person accepts they have sinned. They understand how harmful behaviors have separated them from God. They realize how negativity has affected their life.

6. This person begins to move into self-acceptance, which allows for the healing process to begin.

4th Dimension, Step 1 – Love, Compassion, Forgiveness, Acceptance

1. This person feels they are worthy of self-love.

2. This person believes, "I am a child of Divine Source" and feels the connection.

3. This person has forgiven him or herself, and understands that God and the Masters have also forgiven them.

4. This person feels all is forgiven and understood.

5. This person forgives themselves of their past.

6. This person feels they are part of divine love.

7. This person intends to turn from sin and doesn't perform acts to deceive or injure as they may have done before.

8. This person develops the ability to speak their truth and develops a high self-esteem.

9. This person is willing to accept the serenity prayer, "God, grant me the serenity to accept the things I cannot change, the courage to change the things I can and the wisdom to know the difference."

4th Moving to the 5th Dimension, Step 1 – Love, Compassion, Forgiveness, Acceptance

1. This person can say with confidence, "I love myself and I deserve the very best."

2. This person loves him or herself deeply and completely.

3. This person is full of light and joy.

4. This person forgives him or herself often and moves forward quickly.

5. This person has asked for forgiveness from their enemies, has overcome early childhood traumas and has neutralized their feelings about the experiences.

6. This person's love and compassion has expanded to embrace their family, friends

7. and community.

8. This person's compassion has expanded, and they want to love everyone.

9. This person forgives their sinful past, and begins doing good work.

10. This person has moved into self-acceptance.

11. This person comprehends the affirmation, "I accept things as they are, not as I would like them to be, and in this acceptance, I am free! I am free!"

4. Circle the numbers where you feel the statement is true for you. Make a check mark on the sentences where you know you might need to do some self-reflection.

5. When you compare Step 3 to Step 4, what do you see as the main insight and growth in relationship to self-love? When you compare 4th Moving to the 5th Dimension, what do you see as the main differences. Write down your self-reflection in terms of where you are in your personal spiritual development.

    _____

    _____

    _____

    _____

6. If you feel that you have mastered self-love, you can do this exercise evaluating a client or family member.
    What did you notice is the change in perception between the steps?
    Where would place a client or family member on for Step 1 and how might you assist them to grow in the direction of the next step?

    _____

    _____

    _____

    _____

7. As you move through the material, you may find that you rank very high in some steps, but need to focus on growth in others. The higher up you go in dimensional consciousness, the more your spiritual gifts come in to advance you in your life purpose.

Worksheet 4. *Example Sheet.* Step By Step

Worksheet 4 present an example of how a person moving through self-reflect would answer questions moving step by step through the material. Worksheet 5 is blank. You can make photocopies and move through the material, or use the format for self-reflection in your journal writing.

Each Cosmic Dimension is broken down into steps to help you evaluate different areas of growth in the Ascension process. Use this worksheet to investigate different steps.

Read over the bullet points and make sure it sounds like you. If it does not, adjust. Move up or down in dimensions until you find the correct starting point.

Write in the following information.

What is your Overall Cosmic Dimension _____ *5* _____

Step Number _____ *6* _____

Name of Step _____ *Healing Oneself and Healing Others* _____

Starting Point page number _____ *5th Dim, Step 6* _____

Compare to next step _____ *5th Dim move to 6th, Step 6* _____

QUESTIONS FOR SELF-REFLECTION (OR JOURNAL ENTRY)

1. **What do you notice are the main differences when you compare the two steps?**
    In the first part, the person is starting to work on leading a healthy lifestyle. They are researching and looking for ways to help others. They are working with family and sharing their new healthy lifestyle with others. In the next section, they are healers.

2. **What are the bullet points you are currently working on?**
    In the last year, I have been reading books and investing in new ideas. I really want to help others and I have taken a class in reiki. I want to be more of service to others, but I don't know how.

3. **Write down three goals that will help you get to the next step.**
    I am going to continue to advance my skills and do reiki on myself or others to practice. In the future, I can see myself giving healing to others. I am going to continue looking at other practices.

Worksheet 4. Step By Step

Each Cosmic Dimension is broken down into steps to help you evaluate different areas of growth in the Ascension process. Use this worksheet to investigate different steps. Write in the following information. You could also use this worksheet as a template for a journal entry.

What is your Overall Cosmic Dimension _____

Step Number   _____

Name of Step   _____

Questions for Self-Reflection

1.   What do you notice are the main differences when you compare the two steps?

2.   What are the bullet points you are currently working on?

3.   Write down three goals that will help you get to the next step in dimensional consciousness.

Worksheet 5. Love, Compassion, Forgiveness, Acceptance

Circle the answer that comes closest to your response. Don't overthink your response. Be spontaneous and go with your first impression. Then turn to page 92 for the key to interpret your dimension for Step 1.

1. **When I put my hand over my heart and affirm, "I love myself, I deserve the very best"**
   a) I know I am learning to love myself.
   b) I really want to love myself but feel hurt inside.
   c) I get emotional and start to cry.
   d) Loving myself feels easy, although sometimes others are the priority.

2. **When I consider forgiving my family members, I can honestly say**
   a) I am angry at my family for how I was treated.
   b) I know I need to resolve deep hurts, but it's not a priority for me.
   c) I accept my childhood and have learned how to love myself regardless of the past.
   d) I have done a lot of work to clear subconscious patterns that were modeled to me.

3. **I find myself on the spiritual path because**
   a) I have always been interested in the spiritual path.
   b) I had an experience that opened my heart, now I am curious.
   c) I am in recovery after years of abuse and want to heal.
   d) I have been searching for ways to cultivate self-love in my life.

4. **If I have a conflict with a significant person in my life**
   a) I can see the situation from the other person's point of view.
   b) I often harbor resentment and walk away or start a fight.
   c) I am aware of my anger and I know I want to work this out.
   d) I am quick to forgive and communicate my needs.

5. **When asked to speak to others about a topic I am passionate about**
   a) I am willing to speak up, but afraid I will make a mistake.
   b) I get fearful and wish the responsibility wasn't placed on me.
   c) I feel overwhelmed but know I can speak intelligently.
   d) I believe I can do it, I give it my best shot.

6. **I want love within my heart to expand because**
   a) In light of our differences, I still can love people I don't agree with.
   b) I love all beings everywhere, even if they are dark.
   c) I feel like it's hard to love mean people.
   d) I love my family and friends, but I definitely have problems with some people.

7. **When I am unhappy with my romantic partner**
    a) I feel worthless and shut down, it was probably my fault.
    b) I tolerate a lot of punishment, but I persist in the relationship for many reasons.
    c) There is only so much I can tolerate, and then I draw a line.
    d) I ask the question, "Has the relationship served its purpose?"

8. **If a homeless person asks me for money**
    a) I sometimes give money, other times I wonder if they're deserving.
    b) I use my intuition to decide if I should help this person out.
    c) I normally look away, it's hard for me to consider their suffering.
    d) I feel like it's not my problem, so I don't give money.

9. **When someone tells me I made a mistake**
    a) I immediately blame myself, I always make mistakes.
    b) I can accept feedback and consider if their critique is valid to me.
    c) I feel like I am a terrible person, and nothing goes my way.
    d) I don't care what they think and ignore the message.

10. **When I think about myself**
    a) There are certain aspects of my body that I don't like.
    b) I hate the way my life has gone, my life is a mess.
    c) It's ok with me that I have a unique perspective.
    d) I consider what I like about myself.

11. **When I complete a task that is important to me**
    a) I am my own greatest cheerleader, no matter what, it was great.
    b) I am very hard on myself, I feel like I'm not good enough.
    c) It's good, but not perfect, I could have done better.
    d) As long as I did my best, I am satisfied with my result.

12. **When I look in the mirror, I tell myself.**
    a) I am beautiful inside and out.
    b) I see my imperfections and love myself just the same.
    c) I need to make changes in my life.
    d) I can cover up my f laws and feel beautiful.

Worksheet 6. Forgiveness Issues

THERE ARE NO RIGHT OR WRONG ANSWERS TO THE QUESTIONS.

Answer the questions quickly and spontaneously. It is your emotional response that is being checked, don't overthink it. Answer impulsively and quickly. Circle your answer as A or B. Refer to the key to interpret your Cosmic Dimension, as it relates to forgiveness issues. (Key is located on page 94)

(1) Sometimes I hold grudges (A) or I am quick to forgive (B). . . . . .A or B

(2) Are you in denial of your early childhood trauma (A) or are you over it (B)? . . . . .A or B

(3) Are you angry at any family members (A) or is all forgiven (B)? . . . . .A or B

(4) I sometimes have road rage (A) or I am calm on the road (B). . . . . .A or B

(5) I have problems with some people (A) or I can honestly say I love everyone (B). . .A or B

(6) During an argument I can stay calm (B) or I need to vent and express anger (A). . .A or B

(7) I keep toxic family at a distance (B) or I get involved and am often hurt (A). . . . . .A or B

(8) Is saying "I am sorry" easy for you (B) or very difficult (A)? . . . . .A or B

(9) During a conflict you show remorse first (B) or you prefer to hear an apology (A). . . .A or B

(10) Which is more important during an argument: to be right (A) or to be heard (B)? . .A or B

(11) Do you find it easy (B) or hard to let the past mistakes go (A)? . . . . .A or B

(12) People ask me to listen to them (B) or people know not to bother me (A). . . . . .A or B

(13) Considering my past, I forgive myself (B) or I know I could have done more (A). . .A or B

(14) If I make a mistake, I feel worthless (A) or I learn from my mistakes (B). . . . . .A or B

(15) I asked for forgiveness from God (A) or I have not considered this important (B). . . .A or B

(16) Hurting others ultimately hurts me (B) or some people deserve it (A). . . . . .A or B

(17) During conflicts, I feel misunderstood (A) or conflicts teaches me about myself (B). . . A or B

(18) I counsel people to forgive (B) or I go to counseling to forgive (A). . . . . .A or B

(19) People's behaviors are disrespectful (A) or I tolerate and ignore bad behavior (B). . . .A or B

(20) After a conf lict, it takes days to offer forgiveness (A) or hours (B). . . . . .A or B

Total score: A . . . . B . . . .

Worksheet 7. The 5 Aspects of the Self

To determine your Dimensional Consciousness for Step 2, make a check mark next to the sentence that best describes your attitude towards the physical body.

Physical Body

Low Frequency -1 — This person has little respect for their body and allows it to be unhealthy. This person may disrespect or harm other people physically.

Low Frequency 0 — This person has no respect for their body and chooses to be unhealthy. This person performs acts of self-harm like eating disorders, cutting, or simply doesn't take care of their body. They may have an addiction to alcohol, drugs, sex or food.

Low Frequency 1 — This person may or may not respect their body and may have an addiction.

Low Frequency 2 — This person may or may not exercise and watch their diet. If they desire to improve their physical appearance, it's for worldly pursuits, such as being sexually attractive or advancing in their careers.

3rd Dimension — This person may consider improving their body, but doesn't see physical health as pertaining to spiritual practice.

4th Dimension — This person starts to exercise and watch their diet. This may or may not be done as a spiritual practice.

4th to 5th Dimension — They have a regular routine of exercising. Their diet is clean and they understand the concept of eating high frequency foods.

5th Dimension — This person exercises regularly. They strive to eat higher dimensional foods. They will not eat fast food or processed foods or other man-made foods that are low dimensional.

5th to 6th Dimension — This person has been exercising consistently for some time. They eat high frequency foods.

6th Dimension — This person has almost mastered physical health.

7th to 10th Dimension — This person is a master of their physical body.

My Current Dimension as it relates to the Physical Body is _____

Mental Body

To determine your Dimensional Consciousness for Step 2, make a check mark next to the sentence that best describes your attitude towards the mental body.

Low Frequency -1	This person dwells in negative thinking.
Low Frequency 0	This person is overwhelmed with anger, worry, fear and doubt.
Low Frequency 1	This person has a lot of anger, worry, fear and doubt.
Low Frequency 2	This person may or may not start to illuminate negative thinking and unhealthy thought patterns. Improving thought patterns is motivated by wealth and career advancement. They don't equate disciplining the mind to spirituality.
3rd Dimension	This person may consider changing their negative thought patterns, but doesn't see mental health as pertaining to spiritual practice.
4th Dimension	This person starts to eliminate all negative thinking and unhealthy thought patterns. This may or may not be seen as pertaining to spiritual growth.
4th to 5th Dimension	This person is gaining control over their thoughts, especially of worry and fear. They understand how to quiet their thoughts. This person starts to meditate.
5th Dimension	This person has disciplined their mind. They can recognize if their mind is overactive and quiet their mind. They comprehend that thoughts create reality and, therefore, do not entertain negative thinking.
5th to 6th Dimension	This person has control over their mind and prays and meditates daily.
6th Dimension	This person is healed to an appropriate level physically, mentally, emotionally, energetically and spiritually. This person has balanced their seven chakras. This person understands how to clear their thoughts and use positive affirmations.
7th to 10th Dimension	This person is a master of their 5 Aspects and is modeling or teaching others. They may be a counselor, a life coach or an energy healer.

My Current Dimension as it relates to the Mental Body is _____ .

Emotional Body

To determine your Dimensional Consciousness for Step 2, make a check mark next to the sentence that best describes your attitude towards the emotional body.

Low Frequency -1	This person is emotionally dark.
Low Frequency 0	This person is full of negative emotions and emotional reactivity.
Low Frequency 1	This person has emotional reactivity.
Low Frequency 2	This person may or may not want to gain control over their emotional responses. Usually controlling negative emotions is motivated because of imbalances and relationship difficulties. For example, they notice they have anger management problems and seek help.
3rd Dimension	This person may consider releasing anger and having more control over their emotional reactivity, but doesn't see emotional health as pertaining to spiritual practice.
4th Dimension	This person is gaining control over their emotional responses.
4th to 5th Dimension	This person is gaining control over their thoughts, especially of worry and fear. They understand how to quiet their thoughts. This person starts to meditate.
5th Dimension	This person can calm their emotions. Anger, depression and fear subside. They are quick to forgive, re-center and let go.
5th to 6th Dimension	This person is emotionally self-aware. If they over-react, they immediately pull back towards center.
6th Dimension	This person is healed to an appropriate level physically, mentally, emotionally, energetically and spiritually. This person has control over their emotions and can handle life stresses well.
7th to 10th Dimension	This person is a master of their 5 Aspects and are modeling or teaching others. They may be a counselor, a life coach or an energy healer.

My Current Dimension as it relates to the Emotional Body is _____

Energy/Astral Body

To determine your Dimensional Consciousness for Step 2, make a check mark next to the sentence that best describes your attitude towards the energy/astral body.

Low Frequency -1 to 2	This person is full of negative energy. They are not aware of their energy body.
3rd Dimension	This person may or may not be aware of their energetic or astral body.
4th Dimension	This person recognizes they have an energetic or astral body.
4th to 5th Dimension	This person is aware of the seven chakras, energy healing and the astral realm.
5th Dimension	This person is interested in energy work.
5th to 6th Dimension	This person has cleared their seven chakras. The Light realm is real to them.
6th Dimension	This person is healed to an appropriate level physically, mentally, emotionally, energetically and spiritually. This person has balanced their seven chakras. This person understands how to clear discordant energy through energy work or meditation.
7th to 10th Dimension	This person is a master of their 5 Aspects and are modeling or teaching others.

My Current Dimension as it relates to the Energy/Astral Body is _____

Light Body

To determine your (Dimensional Consciousness) for Step 2, make a check mark next to sentence that best describes your attitude towards your spiritual body.

Low Frequency -1 to 2 This person is not aware of the spiritual aspect of themselves. This person may consider him or herself an atheist or agnostic.

3rd Dimension This person has moved in the direction of understanding they are a spiritual being. They may recognize a formal religious path.

4th Dimension This person believes they came from Divine Source and exists beyond the physical dimension.

4th to 5th Dimension This person understands they are a spiritual being living temporarily in a physical vehicle.

5th Dimension This person considers their life to be spiritually focused.

5th to 6th Dimension This person has cleared their seven chakras. The Light Realm is real to them.

6th Dimension This person is one with Divine Source and can expand their consciousness to new heights.

7th to 10th Dimension This person is a master of their 5 Aspects and are modeling or teaching others. This person is aspiring to be a meditation or spiritual teacher.

My Current Dimension as it relates to the Spirit Body is _____

Worksheet 7 Cont. Self-Reflections

Write Down Your Cosmic Dimension for each of the 5 Aspects.

Physical Body . . . .

Mental Body . . . .

Emotional Body . . . .

Energy/Astral Body . . . .

Spirit Body . . . .

What is your overall Cosmic Dimension for Step Two? Estimate your average.

Physical Body . . . .

Mental Body . . . .

Emotional Body . . . .

Energy/Astral Body . . . .

Spirit Body . . . .

Add total, then divide to your Overall Dimensional Consciousness for Step 2

Which bodies scored higher or lower in dimension?

. . . .

. . . .

What goals might you set in which body aspect, to move up the frequency?

. . . .

Do you feel you have mastered the 5 Aspects or at least are you very close?

. . . .

If you are at high levels of mastery, are you moving towards healing or teaching others?

. . . .

Worksheet 8. Identifying Toxic Friends and Family

CREATING SAFE BOUNDARIES AROUND LOW FREQUENCY PEOPLE

It's safe to create boundaries around toxic friends and family members. As you ascend and are moving up in dimensional consciousness, you start to notice people in your life who bring you down. Often as we embark on the spiritual path, we start to notice an acceleration in growth. Changes start to occur. Activities you once enjoyed no longer feel appropriate, old friends may no longer appeal to you.

Others may find themselves in karmic knots with lower frequency people. Working out unfinished business with others is difficult. A karmic knot is defined as a relationship we wish we could walk away from, but for many reasons cannot. Frequently, we are in karmic knots with family members. This can be the disgruntled ex-wife, the young adult on drugs, or an unloving parent. Any depressed family member is cause for concern. It's hard to live with a family member we know is suffering. **For more information on this, see Chapter 5, Resolving Karma (page 35).**

Earth is a mixed-dimensional environment. Those on the path need to discern which dimension people are. If you find you are surrounded by lower frequency people, you might want to consider making changes, or creating boundaries that make you feel safe. We need to understand when to extend a hand to help someone in need, and when we might be enabling destructive behaviors. It's important that you set the tone of the relationship and on the path of ascension you learn to take the higher road.

Evaluate a toxic friend or family member you know is difficult for you to be in a relationship with. Circle all the answers that come closest to your response.
Don't overthink your response. Be spontaneous and go with your first impression.
Then turn to page 96 for the key on how to deal with a toxic friend or family member.

---

1. **After a long day at work, I come home to a friend or partner who is upset**
   a) They come in angry and get mad about something trivial, later they say they're sorry.
   b) They spend an hour complaining about their experience.
   c) They yell at me and tell me I am the reason they don't like their life.

2. **When talking to this person about school shootings**
   a) They discuss feeling overwhelmed with fear and think school is dangerous.
   b) They discuss why the world has gone crazy and they need to protect themselves.
   c) They identify with the school shooter and laugh or think it is funny.

---

3. **Whenever I am in the same room with this person**
   a)   I feel uncomfortable and my body pulls away from them.
   b)   I feel afraid they might make a comment or start a fight.
   c)   I notice the mood of everyone in the room declines.

4. **At the end of the day, friends or family members**
   a)   Have one alcoholic beverage or smoke to relax.
   b)   Drink a 6 pack or more and drink until they are passed out.
   c)   Drink or smoke a few times a week.

5. **When I get into a fight with this person**
   a)   They get so mad they slam the door or call me names.
   b)   They get so mad we argue and raise our voices until one of us walks away.
   c)   They get so mad they throw something or hit the wall.

6. **Whenever I spend time with this person**
   a)   They tell me they hate their life and start to cry.
   b)   I feel like they take all my positive energy and now I feel depleted.
   c)   I notice self-destructive behaviors and point this out, but they ignore me.

7. **When I am in the car with this person**
   a)   They curse at other drivers and make signals with their hand.
   b)   They get upset very easily, I put up a defensive shield and ignore them.
   c)   They get upset occasionally and this brings my mood down.

8. **In the evening when I spend time with this person**
   a)   I am very careful about how I behave, I am always walking on egg shells.
   b)   They get mad at me about issues, I try to explain, but they overreact in anger.
   c)   As long as we stay away from certain topics, the evening goes well.

9. **This person has a tendency to**
   a)   Be defensive, no matter what I say.
   b)   Pick fights with me for no reason.
   c)   Lash out at me and tell me I am worthless.

10. **After a disagreement with this person**
   a)   They harbor deep-seated resentment and often bring up the past.
   b)   I can feel their anger and am fearful about what they will do.
   c)   I know they will calm down and eventually offer an apology.

11. **You find out this person has lied you.**
    a) I am not surprised; this person is always lying to me, I don't trust them.
    b) I understand why this person lied to me, although I don't approve.
    c) I can't believe the lies and exaggerations.

12. **I understand this person had a difficult childhood**
    a) I excuse bad behavior, it's not all their fault.
    b) I don't want to enable, so I keep my distance.
    c) I know they are trying, and I keep giving them chances.

Worksheet 9. Spiritual Growth towards Ascension

Many people want to develop relations with their angelic teams and move into developing psychic skills. Take the following quiz and find out where you are in your growth towards Ascension. Circle all the answers that come closest to your response, then turn to page 97 to interpret your score.

1. **I practice yoga, meditation, prayer or other forms of spiritual practice**
   a) Every day, I am very dedicated to my spiritual practice.
   b) At least a few times a week, I create space for myself.
   c) I often consider going to practice but it's not a priority for me.

2. **I am interested in exploring concepts on spirituality**
   a) I lead yoga classes or other spiritual groups.
   b) I have read a few metaphysical books.
   c) I work with a spiritual teacher.

3. **I understand the concepts of the energy f low between the hands**
   a) I go to an energy healer for chakra balancing or reiki.
   b) I have seen the chakras on the web, but don't really understand.
   c) I have studied energy healing and have a self-practice.

4. **In terms of daily physical exercise**
   a) I need to start exercising and have a goal to walk during the week.
   b) I am all in when it comes to exercise, I could not live without it.
   c) I enjoy exercise and fit it into my busy schedule when I can.

5. **I have studied spiritual books and spiritual scriptures**
   a) I can recommend several spiritual books to a friend.
   b) I can tell you the name of a book that changed my perspective on spirituality.
   c) I have studied spiritual information in a course and know a lot about the subject.

6. **At night when I go to sleep**
   a) I can't remember my dreams, or I only remember scary dreams.
   b) I may or may not remember my dreams, but I believe I have astral travels and can recall events.
   c) I lucid-dream and explore other realms in dreamtime.

7. I would describe my relationship with Divine Source, my angelic team, or an Ascended Master as
    a) I have defined aspects of my spirituality, and continue to grow and expand.
    b) Clearly defined and understood to me, I feel I can communicate with my guidance team and receive answers back.
    c) I am not sure, it is undefined and ambiguous. I know I am spiritual.

8. During difficult periods in my life, I have
    a) Gone to see a healer or life coach.
    b) Used negative coping skills to handle difficult periods.
    c) Considered finding a healer or life coach but have not gone.

9. When I think about my life purpose
    a) I know exactly what it is. I am motivated and focused and working on manifesting my vision.
    b) I want to know what my life purpose is. I know I have a lot of potential but I'm not sure how to direct my energy.
    c) I have a current direction and I am happy with it, but I am not sure it is my life purpose.

10. I am interested in crystals, divination tools and energy healing
    a) I just took my first course in energy healing.
    b) I have studied healing topics overs the years and can teach what I know.
    c) Whenever a friend comes over, I always offer to give a reading or healing.

11. I often see number signs and experience synchronicities
    a) Recently, I started seeing the angel signs in repeating numbers, it blows my mind.
    b) I have clear communication with my guides through one of my psychic skills.
    c) I wish I could hear my guides.

12. When I meditate
    a) I have a hard time focusing and feel restless.
    b) I "get it", it feels good and expansive, I often receive insights.
    c) I can meditate great with a spiritual teacher or following a guided meditation.

Worksheet 10. Questions for Reflection or Journal Entry

Step 1 - Love, Compassion, Forgiveness and Acceptance

1. Self-love is the entry point to the spiritual path. Describe your attitudes towards loving yourself.
2. Can you identify people in your life you need to forgive? Do you need to ask for forgiveness from someone?
3. Do you think yourself beautiful? Describe your feelings on self-acceptance.
4. Are you too emotionally reactive? Do you carry deep-seated resentment and anger?
5. If you feel you love yourself, is your heart expanded enough to love all beings everywhere?

Step 2 – The 5 Aspects of the Self

1. In relationship to your physical body, what guidance do you receive about changes you need to make to your diet or exercise program?
2. When you move the physical body, do you consider the exercise a spiritual practice?
3. During a stressful event, does your mind assume a positive outcome or a negative outcome? Do you worry too much? Do you know how to calm your thoughts?
4. Can you think of another person that you feel generates negative energy most of time? Can you think of another person that generates positive energy most of the time? How would you describe your energy body? As vibrating positive or negative energy most of the time?
5. How connected do you feel to your "reference point" to God? Reference points to God include your angelic team, an Ascended Master, or your Higher Self. You might also refer to God as the Universe, or spirituality.

Step 3 – Relationship to Family and Community

1. How much of your early childhood do you remember? Have you examined trauma from your early childhood experience? Do you consider yourself healed? Explain.
2. What is your relationship to difficult family members? Do you engage them or do you keep your distance? What are the boundaries of the relationships?
3. Do you have anger management issues? Do you hold grudges? Discuss your relationship with anger in your intimate relationship.
4. Have you or your partner expressed rage at the community (road rage, rage at a public meeting, protest march)?
5. When you consider your circle of love, does it expand beyond your friends and family?

Step 4 – Spiritual Practice and Spiritual Attitude

1. Describe your spiritual background and religious upbringing. How has your spiritual upbringing inf luenced your current spiritual life?
2. What is your current spiritual practice? A spiritual practice is defined as something you do repetitively that is dedicated to your spiritual growth.
3. When you meditate or pray do you feel connected to God? Explain your personal experience and what you receive when you meditate.

4 What is the difference for you between meditation and prayer?

5 What do you consider to be your personal moral code?

Step 5 – Relationship with Divine Source

1 Are you angry with God? If so, why?

2 What direct experiences of God inspired you in the direction of growth and ascension?

3 Describe your relationship with God, or a reference point for God. For example, you may have relationships with your angelic team, your spirit guides, your Lord, Your Ascended Masters, your Guru, your Higher Self, the Oversoul, the Universe or the Galactic Center. You may call God by a different word in your language.

4 When do you most feel the presence of God: in meditation, in nature, in performing an exercise, in going to church, in seeing a spiritual teacher?

5 Do you feel like God listens when you pray, and are your prayers answered?

Step 6 – Healing Oneself and Healing Others

1 How do you share your bright light and love for others in the world?

2 Right now, is your life purpose focused on healing yourself or healing others, or are you working on both at the same time? Explain.

3 When you have been emotionally or physically ill, what positive coping skills or healing practices helped you through the situation? What did you learn from moving through your own healing process?

4 What different healing methods or practices have you studied or would like to study?

5 If a friend or family member comes to you for consultation or healing, what do you do?

Step 7 – Relationship to Humanity and Earth

1 "When I look into other people's eyes, I see light in them." Discuss if this statement is true for you.

2 Do you meditate with the intention of raising the frequency of mass consciousness? In addition to self-expansion, do you pray or meditate for others and the world?

3 Is it important for your vocation to be heart centered and in the healing arts? Or is it more practical for you to keep a monetary vocation and develop a passion project that inspires your heart?

4 What small actions do you perform at home that help you heal the Earth?

5 Do you perform any healing methods or prayers for the Earth, or for the people of the Earth?

Step 8 – Comprehension of the Astral Realms and the Angels

1 What do you believe will happen to you after your spirit leaves your physical body? Are you afraid to die?

2 Do you receive angel signs? Write down signs that you know come from your angelic team.

3 Share your favorite synchronicity story. Explain how you were guided to the happening and why you know it was not a coincidence.

4   Do you know the names of your angels or spirit guides?

5   Do you believe you have encountered an angel along your journey? Do you have a favorite book or story about an angel encounter?

Step 9 – Awakening of Spiritual Gifts and Psychic Powers

1   When you hear a positive voice in your head, do you assume that you are talking to yourself or do you think you could be hearing your intuitive voice?

2   Where are you in terms of trusting yourself when you feel intuitively guided?

3   Do you believe you are an empath? Explain your experiences. Can you sense the energy of people or places? Do you feel like you absorb energy from people and places?

4   Have you developed a language with your angelic guide team that allows you to have direct communication? Are you interested in learning such a language?

5   Do you give psychic readings or work with divination tools to communicate with your angelic team?

Step 10 – Comprehension of the Multi-dimensions

1   When you meditate, can you perceive different levels of depth, or expansion?

2   Are you interested in experiencing spiritual hypnosis or a past-life regression?

3   Are you aware of your activities in dreamtime? Do you lucid dream? Do you receive messages in your dreams? Do you receive visitations from departed love ones in your dreams?

4   Can you feel energy with your hands? Can you run energy through your body? If you practice yoga, do you consider it a physical practice, an energy practice, a spiritual practice or all of these?

5   Do you have an active imagination? Do you spend a fair amount of time daydreaming? Have you considered that you have moved up into a 5th dimensional bubble reality?

Step 11 – Comprehension of the Galactics

1   Do you follow ancient aliens or watch information about the UFOs online?

2   Do you listen to channeled messages? Either from angelic or galactic sources?

3   Do you intuitively know you are a "starseed"? A starseed is a person that believes they are from a different galactic race.

4   Have you, or a friend, ever been abducted or believe you have seen a UFO?

5   Have you ever felt you received an energy healing in dreamtime while you were sleeping?

Key For Worksheet 5 (From Page 75)

Step One – Love, Compassion, Forgiveness, Acceptance

Write in the number that corresponds to your answer, then total the score.
Write down # of your answer

1.	a) 3	b) 1	c) 2	d) 4	
2.	a) 1	b) 2	c) 4	d) 3	
3.	a) 4	b) 2	c) 1	d) 3	
4.	a) 3	b) 1	c) 2	d) 4	
5.	a) 2	b) 1	c) 3	d) 4	
6.	a) 3	b) 4	c) 1	d) 2	
7.	a) 2	b) 1	c) 4	d) 3	
8.	a) 3	b) 4	c) 2	d) 1	
9.	a) 2	b) 4	c) 1	d) 3	
10.	a) 2	b) 1	c) 4	d) 3	
11.	a) 4	b) 1	c) 2	d) 3	
12.	a) 4	b) 3	c) 2	d) 1	

Add the TOTAL SCORE _____

12 - 16   2nd Dimension & 3rd Dimension

Congratulations in taking the first step along the journey to health and happiness! Your curiosity has been piqued or your angelic team has got your attention. You have strong indicators from the universe that it's time to focus on your mission. The journey always begins with an evaluation of your heart. This is an excellent time to seek counseling or self-help programs to help heal your heart.

You may have early childhood trauma that needs to be resolved. There may be outdated subconscious programs that need to be rewritten. If your heart is hurting, seek a healer. It's time to find your spiritual practice and grow your connection in the light. Your angels want to work with you. Take the time and invest in yourself, resolve heart issues and you will quickly fly into the Ascension Dimensions.

17 - 29   4ᵗʰ Dimension

Your life purpose is waiting for you! You know deep down inside that it is time for you to move in the direction of your heart's desires. You have made some progress on the journey but know that you are still working on resolving self-love issues. Take some time to remember what is most important in our life.

Your heart is aware and conscious, now expand that light and develop your heart deeper and wider. Stop making excuses and rekindle your spiritual practice. Learn to love every aspect of yourself. Believe in yourself and tell yourself, "I can do it! I can move in the direction of greatest good and highest happiness."

30 - 33   4ᵗʰ moving to the 5ᵗʰ Dimension

You are definitely growing on your spiritual journey in the direction of complete and total healing on all levels of your being. Keep up the good work. You have been receiving signs and you are on the right path. Continue to expand your studies on metaphysics and healing work. Intend to travel for a healing workshop that

has been calling out to you. You are living life consciously and understanding your own internal thought process. You are centered in your heart and have made tough decisions. Your life is open now to grow in new directions. Continue to expand your heart and move in the direction of your life purpose.

34 - 48   5ᵗʰ Dimension & or Higher

Now is the time to move to the next level in your journey! You feel healed or have made significant progress. Your heart has expanded, and you have completed your healing work. You stand up for yourself and take bold action steps in the direction of your heart purpose. If you are well practiced in a discipline, stay with it. It may be time to start teaching what you

know or learning how to give energy healings. Invest in psychic development and advance your relationship with your angelic team to deepen your healing work. Focus on expanding your practice or learning additional skills to advance your service work. You receive many angel signs on your journey! You are greatly loved and appreciated for your efforts!

KEY for Worksheet 6 (from page 77)

FORGIVENESS ISSUES

Review your total score from Worksheet 3. Use the Total B number and refer to the chart below to find your cosmic dimension in relationship to forgiveness. If you score 20 or more B's, you are spiritually advanced. You have healed your heart and are vibrating in the Higher Frequency dimensions.

If you circled 10 or less B's, you are in the Growth Dimensions and working on forgiveness issues. This is important because forgiveness is linked to karmic issues. Understanding the role of karma is a major theme in this book. Spiritual evolution happens when you open your heart. Forgiveness and self-love are the first steps in the process.

Find a counselor or healer and start to clear heart issues. Work through early childhood trauma and forgiveness issues; clear it and move forward. This creates space in the heart for more love. As you clear, you will rapidly advance in the Cosmic Dimensional scale.

You may feel you have mastered forgiveness issues and have a very compassionate heart. In this case, you are higher frequency and your mission has started or will start soon. When you move into the 5th Cosmic Dimension, you feel healed and ready to progress towards being a healer or a helper.

When you feel a generalized love for all beings everywhere, you know you have moved up in dimensional consciousness. The motto becomes, "To all beings everywhere, love and compassion."

Number of B's

20	High Frequency Dimensions – 7th Dimension or Higher
19-18	Ascension Dimension – 5th Dimension or Higher
17-11	Growth Dimension – 4th moving to the 5th Dimension
10 or less	Growth Dimension – 3rd Dimensional

KEY for Worksheet 8 (from page 84)

Step 3 – Identifying Toxic Friends and Family Members

Write in the number that corresponds to your answer, then total the score. The key below gives suggestion for how to create health boundaries around toxic friends and family members.

1.	a) 3	b) 2	c) 1
2.	a) 2	b) 3	c) 1
3.	a) 1	b) 3	c) 2
4.	a) 3	b) 1	c) 2
5.	a) 2	b) 3	c) 1
6.	a) 3	b) 2	c) 1
7.	a) 1	b) 2	c) 3
8.	a) 2	b) 1	c) 3
9.	a) 3	b) 2	c) 1
10.	a) 2	b) 1	c) 3
11.	a) 1	b) 3	c) 2
12.	a) 2	b) 1	c) 3

Add the TOTAL SCORE _____

12 - 19

This person has a lot of negative energy within them and could be unsafe for you. They usually make you feel stressed out or overwhelmed. People in this range are low frequency. There is energy of bad luck and drama that follows them around. They are quick to anger. There is probably a drug or alcohol problem. Often they are controlling and verbally abusive. If you know someone like this, keep a safe distance. Create strong boundaries. Question the reasons for the relationship or if the relationship has served its purpose. If the person is a family member, you may not be able to get space from them. In this case, shield your auric field and stay non-attached to their self-punishment and self-destructive behavior. Avoid getting in fights with them, don't add fuel to the fire, walk away. Use your best judgement around supporting them financially. You may consider finding a counselor or healer to support you in creating appropriate boundaries or making changes in your life.

20 – 27

This person has a lot of negative energy. They are emotional unhealthy and unhappy with their life. They may have suffered an unexpected job loss, or are unhappy at work. There may be family issues and difficulties handling responsibilities. They have a lot of generalized fear and worry. They may feel trapped in their life. They complain a lot, but are unable to make changes in their life. It could be there was changes in their physical capabilities or an accident. They could have an addiction. Often they are in a sulky or anger mood. If this is a an friend or someone you are in relationship with consider what you are getting out of the relationship, relative to what you put in. This might describe a person you are emotionally disconnected from, but still participating as life partners. As you grow in dimensional consciousness, you may not be able to be with them in their uncomfortable mood. If this person is a family member, be encouraging and help them set goals. Do not take responsibility for their bad choices and avoid enabling them. Encourage them to find a counselor. Set healthy boundaries. Know when to get involved and when to step away.

28-36

This person is lost and confused. They have a limited perceptive on spirituality and lack direction. They may be going through a hard time and their bad mood is effecting everyone they come into contact with. You can tolerate the relationship, but you are on edge. Sometimes they are fine and the next minute they are shouting at you. It's hard to understanding if they are pleased with the relationship or not. They are not totally shut down, but are headed in the wrong direction. They may feel depressed or anxious to you. If you are in a relationship with this person consider couples counseling. Learning how to communicate and becoming self-aware can turn the situation around. Start to observe their mood, they could get better or start to decline. If they are a family member be patience, this may be phase or a difficult transition. Remember your dimensional consciousness relative to theirs. They may not have the same positive coping skills you have or feel supported by the universe. Create healthy boundaries. If they are in a poor mood, stay positive, you don't have absorb their negative energy. If they start a fight, don't engage, don't let them bring your down. Keep up with your positive attitude.

KEY for Worksheet 9 (from page 87)

SPIRITUAL GROWTH TOWARDS ASCENSION

Write in the number that corresponds to your answer, then total the score. The key below indicates where you are in ascent into the Higher Frequencies of Dimensional Consciousness.

1.	a) 3	b) 2	c) 1
2.	a) 3	b) 1	c) 2
3.	a) 2	b) 1	c) 3
4.	a) 1	b) 3	c) 2
5.	a) 2	b) 1	c) 3
6.	a) 1	b) 2	c) 3
7.	a) 2	b) 3	c) 1
8.	a) 3	b) 1	c) 2
9.	a) 3	b) 1	c) 2
10.	a) 1	b) 3	c) 2
11.	a) 2	b) 3	c) 1
12.	a) 1	b) 3	c) 2

Add the TOTAL SCORE _____

12 - 19

Congratulations, you have taken your first steps on the spiritual journey. Discover your passions and receive healing work from others further along on their path. Take a yoga class or find an exercise you enjoy. Dedicate each breath and body movement to becoming you best self. Learn how to meditate. Find a teacher or class that can help you create a bridge to the higher frequency dimensions. You are a beginner in the Ascension process. Ask your angelic team to send you a teacher that can enlighten your journey. Your spirit guides and angels have been calling you to invest in your spiritual growth. You may have started seeing 1111 or 444. This is a signal you have been called for a divine mission and it's time to get to work. You have the ability to expand and you are rapidly growing and changing spiritually. Hold on, spiritual evolution can feel like a roller coaster ride as you clear up the past, and resolve issues of the heart. You are swiftly moving towards ascension.

20 – 27

You have invested in your spiritual journey and are making daily discoveries about your journey. Keep up the good work. Your interest in spiritual topics is awakened and you have found a spiritual instrument that is helping you to develop. That instrument could take many forms. It could be a healer, a guru, or a meditation course. You could have found a book that changed your perspective and helped you to reconsider something. You are open-minded and learning to feel with the antenna on your heart. You are exploring work with divination tools and learning more about your angels. You are qualified to start developing your psychic skills if your gifts are not in already. Participate in a past-life regression session or other form of spiritual hypnosis. You are learning to trust your insights and intuitions.

28 - 36

You are spiritually advanced. You have been on the path for many years and continue to be interested in learning and growing in expanded consciousness. You are either currently a yoga teacher, an energy healer, a life coach, a counselor, or know it is time for you to move in that direction. You may work full-time in a vocation and also have a passion project that keeps you youthful and growing. You know what your spiritual gifts are. You are highly intuitive or may consider yourself psychic. You may give psychic readings to friends with divination tools. You have a strong relationship with your angelic team. You feel supported by the universe and you may support many people in your life.

The Spiritual Guidebook to Ascension

The Lower Frequency Dimensions

-1 DIMENSION - DARKNESS HARM TO OTHERS

This person is evil, malicious and has bad intentions. They are mean-spirited and harm others.

Step 1. Love, Compassion, Forgiveness, Acceptance
1   This person has not yet developed these characteristics.

Step 2. The Five Aspects of the Self
1   This person is lacking in love and is full of hurt, pain and suffering. This person is suffering from addictions.

Physically   This person has little respect for their body and allows it to be unhealthy. This person may disrespect or harm other people physically.

Mentally   This person dwells in negative thinking.

Emotionally   This person is emotionally dark.

Energy/Astral   This person is full of negative energy.

Spiritual   This person has no spirituality, or even a hatred of God. This person may be allied with the dark forces.

Step 3. Relationship to Family and Community
1   This person has usually been hurt or abandoned by family and is deeply angry and wounded.
2   This person is hurt and angry with their community. They have little respect for others in their community or for authority. This person is criminal.

Step 4. Spiritual Practice and Spiritual Attitude
1   This person has no moral code.

2   This person may be dedicated to darkness. They may partake in gang involvement.
3   This person can justify and rationalize their sins against others and the world.
4   This person lives in a hellish reality, full of darkness, hate and anger.

Step 5 to Step 11
1   This person is not yet developed in steps 5 to 11.

0 DIMENSION – DARKNESS HARM TO SELF
This person radiates negative energy and doesn't take care of themselves. They perform acts of self-harm, such as addiction, cutting themselves or developing eating disorders. An addiction or self-harming behavior keeps them in the dark.

Step 1. Love, Compassion, Forgiveness, Acceptance
1   This person may want to be loving but is overwhelmed with negativity.

Step 2. The Five Aspects of the Self
Physically   This person has no respect for their body and chooses to be unhealthy. This person performs acts of self-harm like eating disorders, cutting, or simply doesn't take care of their body. They may have an addiction to alcohol, drugs, sex or food.

Mentally   This person is overwhelmed with anger, worry, fear and doubt.

Emotionally   This person is full of negative emotions and emotional reactivity.

Energy/Astral   This person is not aware of their energetic or astral body. Their primary seven chakras are blocked or withdrawn.

Spiritual   This person is not aware of the spiritual aspect of themselves.

Step 3. Relationship to Family and Community
1 This person has experienced trauma. Their family was broken and abusive.
2 This person is deeply hurt and feels defective.
3 This person is angry with their family or community.

Step 4. Spiritual Practice and Spiritual Attitude
1 This person has a weak moral code and feels life isn't fair.
2 This person is resistant to their life story and may want to end their life.
3 This person lives in a dark reality. They think there is no hope.

Step 5. Relationship to Divine Source
1 This person is angry at God.

Step 6. Healing Oneself and Healing Others
1 This person doesn't want to heal him or herself.

Step 7 to Step 11
1 This person is not yet developed in steps 7 to 11.

1st DIMENSION – DARKNESS UNAWARE OF LIGHT

This person is unaware of the light and has not done self-reflection. They don't care about themselves or the world around them. They don't believe in other realities beyond the 3rd physical dimension. They have a weak moral code.

Step 1. Love, Compassion, Forgiveness, Acceptance
1 This person may experience events that move them from darkness to the light:
2 They survive a suicide attempt.
3 They decline drugs and alcohol and decide there has to be a better way.
4 They get a disease, injury, are victimized, or suffer a trauma that causes them to question.
5 They pray out of desperation and exhaustion for a rescue.

Step 2. The Five Aspects of the Self

Physically   This person may or may not respect their body and may have an addiction.

Mentally   This person has a lot of anger, worry, fear and doubt.

Emotionally   This person has emotional reactivity.

Energy/Astral   This person is not aware of their energetic or astral body. Their primary seven chakras are blocked or withdrawn.

Spiritual   This person is unaware of the spiritual aspect of themselves. This person may consider him or herself an atheist or agnostic.

Step 3. Relationship to Family and Community
1 This person, often hurt by their family, is angry inside. They don't care about their family or community. They exist within their family or community but feel very detached and unappreciative.
2 They may or may not have a relationship with their family. The energies of the family may be dysfunctional, harmful, toxic and full of gossip. Family members feud among themselves or may ignore this person.

Step 4. Spiritual Practice and Spiritual Attitude
1 This person's moral code is weak and therefore it is easy to justify negative habits. Bad habits include viewing pornography, telling lies, stealing small items or money from family and disrespecting family members.
2 This person has a poor attitude at school or work and disrespects authority.
3 This person doesn't understand karma and therefore harming others is of no consequence to them.

Step 5. Relationship to Divine Source
1 This person doesn't believe in God. This person is angry at God.

Step 6. Healing Oneself and Healing Others
1 This person doesn't feel worthy of healing themselves. They feel they deserve to be miserable.

Step 7 to Step 11
1 This person is not yet developed in Steps 7 to 11.

This person believes in God but doesn't feel connected. They are indifferent to the light. Their intention is to satisfy their personal desires. They may or may not show integrity in their moral code. They are a good person and don't harm anyone, although they are self-centered.

Step 1. Love, Compassion, Forgiveness, Acceptance

1 This person may have low self-esteem and may have not learned to love, honor or appreciate themselves.

2 They may feel themselves ugly, worthless or a failure. This person harbors deep roots of resentment. They are unwilling to forgive themselves and others for mistakes they have made in their past.

3 This person knows they are not perfect, but has never asked for forgiveness of their sins. They have never thought it important to clear their karma.

Step 2. The Five Aspects of the Self

1 This person has limited spiritual awareness. They may or may not seek to improve themselves. Oftentimes, they improve themselves for worldly goals and not spiritual goals.

Physically This person may or may not exercise and watch their diet. If they desire to improve their physical appearance, it's for worldly pursuits, such as being sexually attractive or advancing in their careers.

Mentally This person may or may not start to illuminate negative thinking and unhealthy thought patterns. Improving thought patterns is motivated by wealth and career advancement. They don't equate disciplining the mind to spirituality.

Emotionally This person may or may not want to gain control over their emotional responses. Usually controlling negative emotions is motivated because of imbalances

and relationship difficulties. For example, they notice they have anger management problems and seek help.

Energy/Astral This person may or may not be aware of their energy body.

Spiritual This person has a limited perception of God. This person considers themselves an atheist or agnostic.

Step 3. Relationship to Family and Community

1 This person holds grudges and finds it hard to forgive past hurts. This person doesn't understand the value of releasing anger and hurt feelings.

2 This person is angry at family members. This person may seek revenge or be mean to family members.

3 This person may or may not have compassion for the people in their community. They may focus on the negative aspects of the community and complain a lot about what they don't like in their living environment.

4 This person doesn't hold much compassion for the community. Oftentimes, they feel like the world is a mean place and everyone is disrespectful and rude. They can justify being cold in return.

5 This person may or may not have issues with anger. If they have anger issues, this expresses as racism, road rage or having a low tolerance for people who are slower. They may feel peace and joy at times, but these positive feelings are often offset by negative emotions. They are easily overcome by anger, impatience, apathy, meanness, aggressiveness or having a worry-filled mind.

Step 4. Spiritual Practice and Spiritual Attitude

1 This person may be a warm person, however they don't see the value of having a spiritual practice. This person views spirituality as not important or needed in their reality.

2 This person is indifferent about spirituality. It has not occurred to start a spiritual practice. This person may have attended church, but was confused by the experience.

• They don't resonate with the words being used in church, for example, "I am a guilty sinner" or "God needs my worship."

- They have been wounded by people or a situation at church. They don't agree with the message or church practices.
- They feel the focus of the church is on money or building membership rather than on God.

3 They find the topic of spirituality boring and not pleasurable.

4 If they do have a spiritual practice, it is infrequent and not substantive. They go to church only on holidays.

5 This person may or may not consider forgiving others.

6 This person may lead a sinful life and seek the pleasures of the world. This person has sinful habits and doesn't desire to change.

7 This person is aware of the concept of meditation but doesn't understand it.

Step 5. Relationship to Divine Source

1 This person has not yet considered God or the afterlife.

2 This person doesn't have a spiritual teacher.

3 This person feels disconnected from God.

Step 6. Healing Oneself and Healing Others

1 This person may or may not seek to heal themselves. The spiritual aspect of healing is not considered.

2 This person knows they are not healed enough to assist others.

3 This person may or may not want to heal others. Often, if they are a healer or a helper, they have done so out of concern for money or security. For example, a surgeon in the medical environment.

4 This person may want to heal others but hasn't yet healed themselves.

Step 7. Relationship to Humanity and Earth

1 This person may or may not want to heal the Earth. They may take initiatives like recycling, or they may not be considerate at all.

Step 8. Comprehension of the Light Realms and the Angels

1 This person doesn't believe that angels interact with us.

Steps 9 to 11

1 This person is not yet developed in steps 9 to 11.

The Growth Dimensions

3rd DIMENSION – LIMITED PERCEPTIONS OF LIGHT

This person has an understanding of God, learned from a religion. Their perception of God is simplistic. They have not experienced God directly. They are religious and may be open-minded to other truths.

Step 1. Love, Compassion, Forgiveness, Acceptance

1. This person begins to affirm, "I love myself and I deserve the very best." They are moving in the direction of self-love.
2. This person desires to develop love and compassion towards themselves and others. This person begins to move in the direction of understanding compassion.
3. This person moves into the light and asks forgiveness for their sins.
4. This person accepts they have past karma. They understand how harmful behaviors have separated them from God. They realize how negativity has affected their life.
5. This person begins to move into self-acceptance, which allows for the healing process to begin.

Step 2. The Five Aspects of the Self

1. This person wants to better themselves but doesn't view these improvements as being part of spiritual practice.
2. This person is considering giving up addictions.

Physically — This person may consider improving their body, but doesn't see physical health as pertaining to spiritual practice.

Mentally — This person may consider changing their negative thought patterns, but doesn't see mental health as pertaining to spiritual practice.

Emotionally — This person may consider releasing anger and having more control over their emotional reactivity, but doesn't see emotional health as pertaining to spiritual practice.

Energy/Astral — This person may or may not be aware of their energetic or astral body.

Spiritual — This person has moved in the direction of understanding they are a spiritual being. They may recognize a formal religious path.

Step 3. Relationship to Family and Community

1. This person wants to forgive, but may not be able to do so based on hurt feelings.
2. This person seeks to develop compassion and love for other people in their community. This person starts to become aware of anger in their heart and works towards resolving it. This person starts to become aware of anger and emotional over-reactions.
3. This person is introduced to the Fruits of the Spirits. They work in the direction of feeling these attitudes: love, joy, peace, patience, kindness, goodness, gentleness, faithfulness and self-control.

Step 4. Spiritual Practice and Spiritual Attitude

1. This person sincerely wants to heal and improve themselves spiritually. They start a spiritual practice.
2. This person wants to have a relationship with God and actively seeks opportunities to make that happen.
3. This person starts a relationship with God and can connect through prayer and spiritual study, for example, reading the Bible or other scripture.
4. This person becomes aware that spiritual practice includes taking care of themselves and being balanced in their life. They trust their life will change for the better.
5. This person desires to be a good person and follows a conscious moral code of conduct. This person is willing to take an inventory of their sins and weaknesses to work towards correction.
6. This person may or may not understand meditation.

Step 5. Relationship to Divine Source

1. This person highly respects their spiritual teacher. This person feels they are loved as a child of God.
2. This person feels like a relationship has developed with God.

3 This person feels joyful when they participate in church or in a group meditation. This person feels God listens when they pray.

4 This person begins to receive joy from God.

Step 6. Healing Oneself and Healing Others

1 This person becomes aware they need to heal themselves.

2 This person becomes aware of negative behaviors and vices. They contemplate illumination or reduction of bad behavior and addictions.

Step 7. Relationship to Humanity

1 This person wants to be of service in the world and will make a contribution. This person will preach or be a missionary for their specifically chosen path.

2 This person participates in a service mission through their church or another charitable organization.

Step 8. Comprehension of the Light Realms and the Angels

1 This person believes in angels as an abstract concept.

2 This person believes in at least one angel who watches over them, namely their guardian angel.

Step 9 to 11

1 This person is not yet developed in steps 9 to 11.

4th DIMENSION – JOURNEY TO LIGHT

This person is starting their journey into the Light. They study spirituality and have a spiritual practice. They are open to personal growth and meditation. They consider and listen to new ideas before dismissing them. They move into self-love and self-acceptance. This person starts to create a connection to Divine Source.

Step 1. Love, Compassion, Forgiveness, Acceptance

1 This person feels they are worthy of self-love.

2 This person believes, "I am a child of Divine Source" and feels the connection.

3 This person has forgiven themselves and understands that God and the Masters have also forgiven them.

4 This person feels they are part of divine love.

5 This person intends to turn from sin and doesn't perform acts to deceive or injure as they may have done before.

6 This person develops the ability to speak their truth and develops a high self-esteem.

7 This person is willing to accept the serenity prayer, "God, grant me the serenity to accept the things I cannot change, the courage to change the things I can and the wisdom to know the difference."

Step 2. The Five Aspects of the Self

1 This person is working hard to heal themselves physically, mentally, emotionally, energetically and spiritually.

2 They are aware of addictions and seek to purify their life.

Physically This person starts to exercise and watch their diet. This may or may not be done as a spiritual practice.

Mentally This person starts to eliminate all negative thinking and unhealthy thought patterns. This may or may not be seen as pertaining to spiritual growth.

Emotionally This person is gaining control over their emotional responses.

Energy/Astral This person recognizes they have an energetic or astral body.

Spiritual This person believes they came from Divine Source and exist beyond the physical dimension.

Step 3. Relationship to Family and Community

1 This person seeks healing and support from family trauma, so they can move into forgiveness of family.

2 This person begins to communicate with compassion and is working to reduce fighting, especially in their close relationships.

3 This person is working toward loving others in their community through reducing behaviors that are counter to a loving attitude.

4 Love and compassion begin to develop. Their life journey presents opportunities to teach them about developing love in their hearts.

5 This person is less quick to anger.

6 This person reduces using foul language.

7 This person is starting to develop the Fruits of the Spirit: love, peace, patience, kindness, goodness, gentleness, faithfulness and self-control.

Step 4. Spiritual Practice and Spiritual Attitude

1 This person has started a regular spiritual practice like going to church, going into nature, doing yoga, reading spiritual texts, spiritualizing exercise, meditating or going to spiritual groups.

2 This person seeks to have time alone, retreat or go on a spiritual sojourn.

3 This person wants to gain spiritual knowledge and wants to advance spiritually. This person has a strong curiosity and wants to know more.

4 This person has an attitude of forgiveness in their heart.

5 This person has a strong moral code and knows the difference between right and wrong. This person stands in integrity. This person desires to learn how to meditate.

6 This person understands how meditation is different than prayer.

Step 5. Relationship to Divine Source

1 This person seeks spiritual teachers or becomes very committed to a pastor or spiritual representative on their path of mystic teaching.

2 This person, on their own path, is committed to a spiritual study.

3 This person feels connected to Divine Source. They no longer feel a disconnection or a separation. This person starts to feel joy and peace during spiritual attunement.

4 This person feels love in their relationship with Divine Source. This person feels like there is a strong communication with God.

Step 6. Healing Oneself and Healing Others

1 This person is actively working with healers or through self-study to heal.

2 This person is working to heal themselves completely. This person is working actively to change their diet, clear childhood issues, make amends, start to exercise and stop bad habits.

3 This person starts to seek out healers and gains experience about healing.

4 This person starts to approach purification. They understand they need to purify the Five Aspects of Self for spiritual development. They become aware of how these aspects impede their spiritual progress.

5 This person investigates healing arts and services they may be interested in performing.

6 This person seeks to increase their knowledge base about being a healer or helper in the world.

Step 7. Relationship to Humanity

1 This person expands their perception from ego concerns to humanity concerns. This person wants to serve humanity.

2 This person becomes aware of the concept of mass consciousness.

3 This person may start to consider issues of pollution and how it is affecting our Earth.

Step 8. Comprehension of the Light Realms and the Angels

1 This person believes in angels.

2 This person is fascinated with the idea of angels and reads books and stories about them. This person starts to study the subject of angels, Light Realms and the Divine Masters. This person believes that angels are guiding their path.

Step 9. Awakening of Spiritual Gifts and Psychic Powers

1 This person starts to experience synchronicities.

2 This person may start to see repeating number patterns such as 444 and 11-11. This person may feel intuitive and guided by Angels, Masters or Divine Source. This person may see a psychic reader.

3 This person is interested in psychic development.

Step 10. Comprehension of the Multi-Dimensions

1 This person will investigate multi-dimensional concepts, mostly through reading books and attending workshops.

2 This person, through meditation practice, may feel they are moving into deeper levels of trance. This person may or may not understand energy work.

Step 11. Comprehension of the Galactic

1 This person feels they are out of place.

2 This person may or may not be interested in Galactic and UFO information.

4th MOVING TO THE 5TH DIMENSION - DOORWAYS TO LIGHT

This person is working in the direction of complete healing. They have opened many doorways to light. Open-minded experience has brought new awareness. They are learning meditation. They have experienced a feeling of connection to Divine Source.

Step 1. Love, Compassion, Forgiveness, Acceptance

1   This person can say with confidence, "I love myself and I deserve the very best." This person loves him or herself deeply and completely.

2   This person forgives him or herself often and moves forward quickly.

3   This person has overcome early childhood traumas and neutralized their feelings about the experiences.

4   This person's love and compassion has expanded to embrace their family, friends and community. This person's compassion has expanded, and they want to love everyone.

5   This person has moved into self-acceptance. This person comprehends the affirmation, "I accept things as they are, not as I would like them to be and, in this acceptance, I am free! I am free!"

Step 2. The Five Aspects of the Self

1   This person has worked on themselves and made progress. They have made gains in their health and understand healing as a spiritual practice.

Physically   They have a regular routine of exercising. Their diet is clean, and they understand the concept of eating high-dimensional foods.

Mentally   This person is gaining control over their thoughts, especially of worry and fear. They understand how to quiet their thoughts. This person starts to meditate.

Emotionally   This person continues to gain control over their emotional responses.

Energy/Astral   This person is aware of the seven chakras, energy healing and the astral realm.

Spiritual   This person understands they are a spiritual being living temporarily in a physical vehicle.

Step 3. Relationship to Family and Community

1   This person begins to perceive all people as containing divine light. This person starts identifying negative people.

2   Negative family members are held at a distance and with appropriate boundaries.

3   This person wants to move toward a positive vocation. They take steps to move out of a negative work environment.

4   This person wants to move out of a negative location at home or where they live. They take steps to create a new landscape for their reality.

5   This person has a genuine respect and kindness for people they see in their community but do not know.

6   This person continues to work on their anger response. They may still get angry, but quickly forgive and come back to center.

7   The Fruits of the Spirit continue to grow and develop: love, peace, patience, kindness, goodness, gentleness, faithfulness and self-control.

Step 4. Spiritual Practice and Spiritual Attitude

1   This person practices spiritual tolerance of all faiths. This person feels connected to their Master(s).

2   This person uses positive affirmations, Bible verses, prayers, joyful praises and mantras. This person forgives themselves and others easily.

3   This person may seek to participate in a spiritual community. This person may decide they want to be monastic.

4   This person seeks significant change in the direction of a joyful life. This person has a strong moral code.

5   This person begins daily meditation, prayer or finds quiet time for self-contemplation. This person starts to understand the difference between prayer and meditation.

Step 5. Relationship to Divine Source

1   This person identifies with one or several spiritual teachers. This person feels joy through being present in the world. This person starts to feel joy during spiritual attunement.

2   This person starts to feel joy in everyday life doing ordinary tasks.

3   This person feels connected to Divine Source. A relationship is established.

Step 6. Healing Oneself and Healing Others

1 This person wants to heal themselves. Through the healing process, they have experienced healing techniques and have gained insight about how they might serve the world.

2 This person has one or two obstacles left before they feel completely healed. This person is studying the healing arts, and this may continue for several years. This person wants to know their life purpose.

Step 7. Relationship to Humanity

1 This person investigates occupations that involve heart attitudes like helping, healing, or producing healthy products.

2 This person is beginning to understand how media is a distraction from spiritual pursuits. This person takes small practical actions to help heal the Earth.

Step 8. Comprehension of the Light Realms and the Angels

1 This person knows their angels or Masters surrounding them.

2 This person knows a family member is watching over them as an angel.

3 This person notices coincidence and other signs that the Light Realm is real and attempting to get their attention. Synchronicities start occurring for them.

Step 9. Awakening of Spiritual Gifts and Psychic Powers

1 This person investigates psychic topics through books and workshops. This person starts to play with divination tools.

2 This person has intuitions about people, places and situations. This person notices they are empathic and sensitive to energy.

3 This person may begin reading or listening to channeled information. This person investigates forms of trance through hypnosis, spiritual ceremony, sound vibration or other methods of trance.

4 This person starts to realize the concept of present moment consciousness.

Step 11. Comprehension of the Galactic

1 This person is fascinated with ancient aliens or galactic investigations. This person follows alien topics or channeled messages on the Internet.

2 This person resonates with the affirmation, "I am in the world, but not of the world."

The Ascension Dimensions

5th DIMENSION –
LIGHT REALMS CHRIST CONSCIOUSNESS

This person is connected to and receiving love from Divine Source. They are walking the spiritual path of Christ Consciousness. They are expanding in love. They recognize oneness in everyone. If they choose to awaken spiritual gifts, they develop intuition. They are receiving divine guidance and are happy with life. They are healed and every day is a good day.

Step 1. Love, Compassion, Forgiveness, Acceptance

1. This person's compassion has expanded, and they love everyone. This person knows we all come from love.
2. This person has expanded from self-love to all beings everywhere, love and compassion. This person has completely forgiven themselves.
3. This person practices forgiveness of others. This person accepts themselves as they are.
4. This person accepts their karma with loving grace. This person accepts divine timing.

Step 2. The Five Aspects of the Self

1. This person is healed and has released all addictions.

Physically   This person exercises regularly. They strive to eat higher dimensional foods. They will not eat fast food or processed foods or may choose not to eat meat.

Mentally   This person has disciplined their mind. They can recognize if their mind is overactive and can quiet their mind. They comprehend that thoughts create reality and therefore, do not entertain negative thinking.

Emotionally   This person can calm their emotions. Anger, depression and fear subside. They are quick to forgive, re-center and let go.

Energy/Light   This person is interested in energy work.

Spiritual   This person considers their life to be spiritually focused.

Step 3. Relationship to Family and Community

1. This person is distant from unhealthy family and friends.
2. This person is quick to forgive others, no matter the situation or environment.
3. This person loses interest in negatively charged environments, for example, a bar or nightclub. This person sees all people containing Divine light.
4. This person releases anger quickly.
5. This person starts to understand unity consciousness.
6. The Fruits of the Spirit comes forward: love, joy, peace, patience, kindness, goodness, gentleness, faithfulness and self-control.

Step 4. Spiritual Practice and Spiritual Attitude

1. This person has a strong and regular spiritual practice. This person is open to different spiritual communities. This person's daily experience is joyful.
2. This person practices forgiveness.
3. This person understands that hurting others is ultimately hurting oneself. This person abides by a strong moral code.
4. This person's meditation practice is strong and practiced daily.
5. This person practices mindfulness and present-moment consciousness.

Step 5. Relationship to Divine Source

1. This person receives joy and wants to share it with others. This person has a strong relationship with Divine Source.
2. This person feels Divine Source is everywhere and in everyone. This person knows that Divine Source is listening to them.

Step 6. Healing Oneself and Healing Others

1. This person assists others in leading a healthy lifestyle. This person researches new ways to improve their health.
2. This person feels ready to serve and is looking for opportunities to practice. This person may know their

life purpose or be praying to discover it. This person wants to be of service in the world. This person wants to help heal the Earth.

3   This person shares wisdom with family and friends. This person is practicing their new healing skills.

Step 7.   Relationship to Humanity

1   This person loves humanity and wants to give to the world.

2   This person feels they are expanding beyond formal religious concepts. This person prays to end all religious war and in-fighting.

3   This person understands the media is biased towards capitalistic interest.

4   This person is conscious their purpose involves healing people and healing the Earth.

Step 8.   Comprehension of the Light Realms and the Angels

1   This person notices when angels comfort them.

2   This person knows angels communicate through symbols and signs.

3   This person notices 444 and 1111 frequently. They believe it's meaningful to their life purpose. This person contemplates the synchronicities and feels encouraged to take action.

4   This person asks for assistance from their angels and notices the signs.

5   This person knows their angels are guiding them to their highest happiness.

Step 9.   Awakening of Spiritual Gifts and Psychic Powers

1   This person desires spiritual gifts and psychic powers from Divine Source.

2   This person is interested in divination tools: angel cards, pendulum, crystals, runes, I-Ching, tea leaf reading, dowsing rods, sacred geometry, sacred space, other types of cultural readings and symbols.

3   This person is sensitive to other people's energy.

4   This person's energy declines in public spaces like shopping centers or stadiums. This person begins listening to channeled information on the internet.

Step 10. Comprehension of the Multi-Dimensions

1   This person is mindful in ordinary moments.

2   This person distinguishes between levels of trance. This person understands all matter is energy.

3   This person researches the chakras.

4   This person is interested in energy healing.

5   This person is interested in sound healing, vibrating a bowl or using tuning forks. This person is interested in spiritual hypnosis.

6   This person educates themselves on multi-dimensional topics.

7   This person resonates with the concept that they are a Light Worker.

Step 11. Comprehension of the Galactics

1   This person wonders what they are doing on this planet. This person feels the world is too violent for their energy. This person believes humans are not alone.

2   This person identifies with Indigo, Crystalline, Rainbow, Starseed, Wanderer or Galactic.

5th MOVING TO THE 6th DIMENSION – LIGHT REALMS LIGHT WORKER

This person is learning a healing technique and wants to serve the world. They are conscious they are Lightworkers. They bring light to the dark world. Their actions are loving and compassionate. Intuition is strong. They know how to connect to Divine Source. They begin to develop psychic skills. They are opening to multi-dimensionality.

Step 1.   Love, Compassion, Forgiveness, Acceptance

1   This person understands Christ Consciousness.

2   This person teaches "to all beings everywhere, love and compassion."

3   This person has compassion for lower-frequency people and credulity in the world.

4   This person practices forgiveness of others, even those they have never known personally. This person believes we are all from Divine Source and can see the Divine spark in everyone. This person is a child of Divine Source, full of love and joy. This person has mastered forgiveness.

5   This person has mastered self-acceptance. This person accepts all people.

6   This person accepts their community and the world.

Step 2. The Five Aspects of the Self

1   This person is healed and has released all addictions. They are purified and cleansed in the five bodies.

Physically   This person has been exercising consistently for some time. They eat high frequency foods.

Mentally   This person has control over their mind and prays and meditates daily.

Emotionally   This person is emotionally self-aware. If they over-react, they immediately pull back towards center.

Energy/Light   This person know how to clear their seven chakras. The Light Realm is real to them.

Spiritual   This person is one with Divine Source and can expand their consciousness.

Step 3. Relationship to Family and Community

1   This person spends their time in positive environments, with positive friends and loving people. This person loves the world.

2   This person sees all people containing Divine light, even the darkest among us. This person no longer struggles with anger and their family and community. This person realizes Christ Consciousness.

3   This person realizes unity consciousness.

4   The Fruit of the Spirit bears fruit and is realized and shared with others.

Step 4. Spiritual Practice and Spiritual Attitude

1   This person is on the path of enlightenment.

2   This person's spiritual practice extends to ordinary moments in life.

3   This person's spiritual practice exists in present-moment consciousness. Nothing is pushed away or resisted. This person forgives as a way of life.

4   This person views all obstacles as a teaching tool for spiritual growth.

5   This person wants all people to find a path to connect them to Divine Source. This person sees the light in a person rather than their religious title.

6   This person leads others in meditation.

Step 5. Relationship to Divine Source

1   This person honors all spiritual representatives of Divine Source. This person is one with Divine Source.

2   This person is in unity with the world. This person loves all living creatures.

3   This person feels Divine Source so abundantly they vibrate this consciousness to the planet. This person feels joyful every day.

4   This person has an abundance of joy overflowing. They give joy to others. This person receives their mission from Divine Source.

5   This person communicates with Divine Source.

Step 6. Healing Oneself and Healing Others

1   This person is healed and ready to assist others.

2   This person has studied many healing techniques and styles.

3   This person continues to expand their insight in the healing arts. This person is considered a novice in their healing practice.

4   This person feels ready to serve and opportunities start to present themselves. This person practices different healing skills.

Step 7. Relationship to Humanity

1   This person is expanded beyond their self-interest and recognizes they are a part of humanity. This person knows how important their service is to humanity.

2   This person works toward manifesting a new vocation that resonates with their heart. This person's vocation becomes uncomfortable if the only focus is making money. This person may find a passion, in addition to their vocation, that fulfills their heart. This person affects mass consciousness one person at a time.

Step 8. Comprehension of the Light Realms and the Angels

1   This person believes angels are interacting with them.

2   This person notices synchronicities are frequent and beyond coincidence.

3   This person asks for assistance from their angels and takes action when doors open. This person reads stories about angels.

4   This person recalls phrases and affirmations sent from the angels throughout the day. This person may see colors when meditating.

Step 9. Awakening of Spiritual Gifts and Psychic Powers

1. This person develops spiritual gifts through a spiritual practice like yoga or meditation. This person plays with different divination tools.
2. This person's intuition develops.
3. This person feels the energy of people, places and things.
4. This person is highly emotional and doesn't understand why they are overrun by their emotions.
5. They may feel they are empathic.
6. This person believes they receive information in dreams. This person is interested in learning how to channel. This person desires to give psychic readings.

Step 10. Comprehension of the Multi-Dimensions

1. This person experiences trance states frequently.
2. This person is conscious their mind is different than their Lightbody.
3. This person listens to chants, mantras and toning. They notice how vibration affects their consciousness.
4. This person feels their auric field.
5. This person goes to an energy healer to experience divine energy flow. This person studies pranic healing and other energy-healing techniques. This person studies spiritual hypnosis.

Step 11. Galactic Comprehension

1. This person is interested in ancient aliens and galactic topics. This person is interested in crop circles.

6th DIMENSION – LIGHT REALMS AWARENESS

This person has a strong connection to Divine Source. Their awareness opens to new dimensions. Spiritual gifts and psychic skills begin to develop. They walk in truth and light. They are open to multi-dimensional concepts. They are becoming healers and spiritual teachers.

Step 1. Love, Compassion, Forgiveness, Acceptance

1. This person has almost mastered Step 1.
2. This person is qualified to be a spiritual teacher. This person helps others forgive.

3. This person sees the Divine Source in everyone.
4. This person stays centered even during unsettling events.

Step 2. The Five Aspects of the Self

1. This person is healed to an appropriate level physically, mentally, emotionally, energetically and spiritually. This person has balanced their seven chakras. This person understands how to clear their thoughts and use positive affirmations.
2. This person understands how to clear discordant energy through energy work or meditation. This person understands they are primarily a spiritual being and the other components wrap around and complete them.

Step 3. Relationship to Family and Community

1. This person has almost mastered loving family and community. This person loves everyone and sees all as Divine sparks.
2. This person releases anger immediately and forgives quickly. This person is qualified to be a spiritual teacher.
3. This person is advanced in their spiritual practice and spiritual attitude. This person's spiritual practice radiates outward to the world.
4. This person teaches others all obstacles are tools for spiritual growth. This person has a strong meditation practice.

Step 5. Relationship to Divine Source

1. This person is a spiritual representative of Divine Source. This person radiates joy.
2. This person starts working on their mission and that brings them joy. This person communicates about Divine Source.

Step 6. Healing Oneself and Healing Others

1. This person integrates different methods they know from studying the healing arts. This person starts to present as a healer in the world.
2. This person is confident they can help, if others are ready to heal.

Step 7. Relationship to Humanity and Earth

1. This person understands each is on their own path.
2. This person accepts that religion is organized by humans and is therefore f lawed.

3　This person is manifesting a new career that has a positive relationship with humanity and the Earth.

4　This person is aware of corporate manipulation.

5　This person hopes all humans will participate in healing the Earth. This person takes small action steps daily to heal the world.

6　This person participates in activities to help Earth.

7　This person understands that groups of people create a "group" dimensional consciousness. This person understands that all humans create a "mass" dimensional consciousness.

8　This person is aware mass consciousness is ascending.

Step 8.　Comprehension of the Light Realms and the Angels

1　This person may become aware of the name of the angel or guide they are working with. This person receives intuitive thoughts from their angels like whispers.

2　This person reads angel cards or receives messages through other divination tools. This person can see, sense, feel or imagine their angels during hypnosis.

3　This person is starting to see, sense, feel or imagine their angels in meditation. This person creates their own affirmations inspired by the angels.

4　This person starts to take an interest in a Master as well as angels.

Step 9.　Awakening of Spiritual Gifts and Psychic Powers

1　This person receives spiritual gifts from Divine Source and the Masters. This person explores psychic development through mentors and workshops.

2　This person opens to telepathy. They will receive an intuition before a friend calls or will know something a few minutes before it happens.

3　This person recognizes they are an empath and sensitive to energy. This person notices changes in their energy level during the day. This person is interested in the meaning of dreams and astral travel. This person is interested in dreamtime.

4　This person manifests through intention and prayer. This person comprehends thoughts create reality.

Step 10.　Comprehension of the Multi-Dimensions

1　This person chooses to be fully present in the moment.

2　This person moves from exploring trance to becoming multi-dimensional. This person notices how vibrations like AUM affect consciousness.

3　This person is conscious their mind is different than their Higher Self. This person practices an energy exercise like yoga, tai chi or qi gong. This person can feel prana (divine energy) through their hands.

4　This person is interested in the energy body and the auric field. This person believes in reincarnation.

5　This person is interested in spiritual hypnosis or past-life regression. This person notices their world view is different from others.

6　This person comprehends the universe is vast and has intelligent life. This person studies ancient aliens and galactic topics.

The Higher Frequency Dimensions

7th DIMENSION –
LIGHT REALMS LIGHT OF THE ANGELS

This person services the light and is working with their angels. They are further along in their spiritual practice and growth. They love everyone. They bridge to the astral dimensions. They may start to become aware of the galactic realms. They focus primarily on spiritual concerns.

Step 1. Love, Compassion, Forgiveness, Acceptance
1 This person has mastered Step 1.

Step 2. The 5 Aspects of the Self
1 This person is healed in all aspects of their being.

Step 3. Relationship to Family and Community
1 This person may choose to work in the world, and serves everyone.
2 This person may choose to become a renunciant and seek monastic life. This person seeks to raise the cosmic dimensions of the entire world. This person has mastered all aspects of loving family and community.

Step 4. Spiritual Practice and Spiritual Attitude
1 This person is a spiritual teacher and works in the world, teaching what they know. If this person is monastic, they are fully engrossed in spiritual practice.
2 This person leads group meditation and the group radiates peace out to the world. This person is one with unity consciousness. This person is attuned to Divine Source.
3 This person honors all representatives of Divine Source.

Step 6. Healing Oneself and Healing Others
1 This person has integrated healing studies to create a unique style. This person is known as a healer.
2 This person helps others find their life purpose.

Step 7. Relationship to Humanity and Earth
1 This person recognizes the light in a person rather than the religious path. This person finds themselves in the role of healer or helper to the world. This person's life purpose keeps them busy in the world.
2 This person services other people with a generous heart. This person is aware of the Ascension process.

Step 8. Comprehension of the Light Realms and the Angels
1 This person allows for more angels to work with them.
2 This person knows angels and Masters are guiding their path.
3 This person invites an Earth or Light Realm Master into their heart chakra. This person's Master directs their spiritual growth.
4 This person feels the different personalities of their angels or Masters.
5 This person experiences joy when meditating with the Master of their heart.
6 This person's ability to see, sense, feel or imagine in meditation improves. They can experience their angels more clearly.

Step 9. Awakening of Spiritual Gifts and Psychic Powers
1 This person's spiritual gifts and psychic powers begin to develop.
2 This person starts to develop the ability to visualize and trust intuition. This person utilizes divination tools to communicate with angels.
3 This person has intuitions about people, places and events.
4 This person is aware they are an empath and discerns their energy from the energy of others. This person is interested in dream interpretations and astral travel.
5 This person is aware one co-creates their life based on intention. This person starts channeling messages themselves.

Step 10. Comprehension of the Multi-Dimensions
1 This person goes into trance listening to theta music. This person goes into trance during spiritual ceremony.
2 This person's meditation advances to expand their Lightbody. This person learns how to lead others in meditation.
3 This person begins to feel or see auras. This person studies the chakra system.

4 This person uses a form of sound healing or vibration to perform energy healing. This person moves divine energy through their body.

5 This person studies pranic energy healing.

6 This person can feel if their chakras are blocked. This person seeks a spiritual hypnosis experience.

7 This person communicates with their Higher Self in hypnosis.

8 This person knows going to a movie theater is similar to traveling into another dimension.

Step 11. Galactic Comprehension

1 This person strongly believes we are not alone. This person resonates with being a "volunteer".

2 This person believes crop circles are a sign of intelligent life.

3 This person seeks communities identified as Indigo, Crystalline, Rainbow, Starseed or Galactic.

8th DIMENSION – LIGHT REALMS I AM THAT

This person is advanced on their spiritual path. I AM THAT refers to their knowingness they are one with Divine Source. Their spiritual gifts and psychic powers are expanding. They are recognized as a representative of Divine Source. They are multi-dimensional beings.

Step 1. Love, Compassion, Forgiveness, Acceptance

1 This person has mastered Step 1.

Step 2. The Five Aspects of the Self

1 This person is healed on all aspects of their being.

2 This person exists in a state of grace; they are happy and relaxed every day.

Step 3. Relationship to Family and Community

1 This person raises the consciousness of the world.

2 This person has mastered all aspects of loving family and community.

Step 4. Spiritual Practice and Spiritual Attitude

1 This person's high dimensional consciousness shifts the vibration of the world.

Step 5. Relationship to Divine Source

1 This person feels they are one with Divine Source.

Step 6. Healing Oneself and Healing Others

1 This person expands their healing work.

Step 7. Relationship to Humanity and Earth

1 This person moves away from earthly interests and desires.

2 This person perceives all as containing light, regardless of their consciousness. This person utilizes spiritual gifts in their vocation.

3 This person has a simple life.

4 This person seeks to raise the vibration of mass consciousness through meditation and healing efforts.

5 This person raises the mass consciousness towards Ascension.

Step 8. Comprehension of the Light Realms and the Angels

1 This person gains new spiritual insight.

2 This person receives intuitive thoughts from their Masters like whispers.

3 This person receives knowledge from books written by students of the Masters. This person is guided by angels and Masters.

4 This person explains spiritual principles to others.

5 This person understands that angels support them and Masters give knowledge.

6 This person contemplates all angels and Masters are individuals and all are one with Divine Source. This person knows the energy of the Masters in their heart.

Step 9. Awakening of Spiritual Gifts and Psychic Powers

1 This person's spiritual gifts and psychic powers continue to develop.

2 This person starts to develop clairvoyance, clairaudience and clairsentience. This person feels telepathic with close friends or family.

3 This person knows they are an empath and can feel the energy of people, places and situations. This person manifests and allows for divine timing.

4 This person keeps a dream journal and asks for messages to come in their dreams. This person intentionally travels in dreamtime.

Step 10. Comprehension of the Multi-Dimensions

1. This person uses rhythm and drumming to open to trance states.
2. This person chants, repeats mantras or toning vibrations to go into trance states. This person understands how their Lightbody and Higherself are related.
3. This person clears their chakras 1-7 through different methods.
4. This person directs prana (divine energy) through their chakras for balanced energy f low. This person has experienced a couple of spiritual hypnosis sessions.
5. This person is interested in astral travel, the Akashic Records and the unconscious.
6. This person knows their imagination is a non-physical dimension, rather than an unreal dimension. This person prefers high-dimensional places, situations and objects.

Step 11. Galactic Comprehension

1. This person knows their world view is different than others. This person wants to communicate with galactics.

9th DIMENSION – LIGHT REALMS ONENESS

This person practices "oneness" and feels unity between all beings. This person is a spiritual teacher of teachers. They are spiritual leaders within their communities. They may participate in the astral realms and galactic realms. They have a multitude of spiritual gifts. Their Masters have taken an interest in them and are guiding them.

Steps 1-6

1. This person has mastered the first Six Steps and are healers in the world.

Step 7. Relationship to Humanity and Earth

1. This person realizes unity consciousness. This person recognizes we are all one. This person is one with humanity and Earth.
2. This person knows all spiritual paths lead to Divine Source. Forgiveness is granted to all beings everywhere.

3. This person takes action as a Light Worker.
4. This person, if monastic, will retreat from the world.
5. This person affects mass consciousness through meditation. This person meditates for world ascension.

Step 8. Comprehension of the Light Realms and the Angels

1. This person seeks knowledge from their Masters. This person studies books about their Masters.
2. This person creates a bridge between the physical realm and the Light Realms. This person requests Masters lead them towards spiritual goals.
3. This person becomes a representative of their Masters.
4. This person has expanded their team of angels and Masters.
5. This person experiences attunement with the Master of their heart. This person receives intuitive knowledge from their Masters.
6. This person knows telepathic thoughts come from angels and Masters.

Step 9. Awakening of Spiritual Gifts and Psychic Powers

1. This person's spiritual gifts and psychic powers are advancing. This person has telepathic moments with friends and family. This person receives messages in their dreams.
2. This person develops a beautiful meditation or hypnosis voice. This person develops patience when manifesting in divine timing. This person can channel messages from angels.
3. This person gives psychic readings.

Step 10. Comprehension of the Multi-Dimensions

1. This person connects their Lightbody and Higher Self to the other aspects of themselves. This person expands their Lightbody during meditation.
2. This person clears their higher chakras unconsciously through meditation. This person begins to f low prana though others. This person feels the auric field of another.
3. This person directs pranic energy through other people's bodies.
4. This person is interested in leading others in spiritual hypnosis or visualization. This person wants to associate with other Lightworkers.

Step 11. Comprehension of the Galactic

1. This person believes we are not alone and has some connection with galactics. This person has an advanced study in ancient aliens and galactics.
2. This person may listen to channeled messages from galactics.

10th DIMENSION – DOORWAYS TO DIVINE SOURCE

This person is a doorway to Divine Source. They hear, sense or communicate with their angels and Masters directly. Their spiritual gifts and psychic powers are known to them and they are working towards mastery.

Steps 1-6

1. This person has mastered the first Six Steps and are healers in the world.

Step 7. Relationship to Humanity and Earth

1. This person's main focus is service to humanity and Earth. This person's primary focus is their mission.
2. This person is clear about their life purpose and how to serve in the world. This person knows Earth is infinite and human existence is temporary.
3. This person knows humans are a part of mass consciousness and have power to affect the whole. This person understands Divine Source sent Lightworkers to assist with Ascension.

Step 8. Comprehension of the Light Realms and the Angels

1. This person invites a Master into their crown chakra.
2. This person asks the Masters to guide their mission and life purpose. This person represents the Masters and Divine Source.
3. This person hears thoughts from angels and Masters.
4. This person teaches the wisdom of their Masters or spiritual path.

Step 9. Awakening of Spiritual Gifts and Psychic Powers

1. This person knows they are strongly psychic.
2. This person is clairvoyant, clairaudient and clairsentient. This person is skilled in their divination practice.
3. This person is becoming telepathic.
4. This person sets an intention for experience in dreamtime. This person knows all comes in divine timing.
5. This person channels messages from angels.

Step 10. Comprehension of the Multi-Dimensions

1. This person can move into different trance states.
2. This person experiences trance and other multi-dimensions. This person sees and feels auras.
3. This person clears their higher chakras consciously.
4. This person understands all matter is energy, and all energy is Divine Source. This person seeks training to perform spiritual hypnosis and past-life regression. This person practices leading hypnosis.
5. This person can give past-life readings or retrieve information from the Akashic records. This person teaches other Lightworkers.

Step 11. Comprehension of the Galactic

1. This person identifies with a specific galactic origin, like Pleiadians, Sirian, or Orion. This person serves humanity as a galactic volunteer.
2. This person believes galactics interact with humans.

Glossary of Terms for the 10 Cosmic Dimensions

ANGELS LIGHT
Beings that dwell in the Light Realms and serve on Earth to assist humans during their journey in physicality.

ASTRODOME
The physical universe that humans dwell in, containing galaxies, planets, suns, stars and space.

ASCENSION, HUMAN
A human spiritual evolution where humans ascend to 5th dimensional consciousness or higher.

ASCENSION, INDIVIDUAL
An individual's spiritual evolution where one progresses from one dimension to higher dimensions.

ASCENSION SYMPTOMS
An adverse effect occurring when the Cosmic Ray is at, or near, maximum levels. Ascension symptoms include headaches, fatigue and withdrawal. One's life story may be significantly adjusted, for example, ending a job or relationship. Lightworkers are adjusting to higher dimensions.

ATTUNEMENT
Matching one's consciousness to a higher dimensional source.

AURIC FIELD
A component of the Energy Body. A field of energy around the physical body.

CHAKRAS, 1-7
A component of the Energy Body. A chakra is a spinning center of energy containing positive and negative emotions and energies. There are 7 major chakras located in the human body.

CHAKRAS, 100
A component of the Energy Body. A chakra is a spinning center of energy containing positive and negative emotions and energies. There are 100 chakras in one's divine line connecting one to Divine Source.

CHANNELING
A communication link to astral beings where information is shared.

CONSCIOUSNESS, CHRIST
A person whose consciousness is expanded to embrace all with love and compassion. A person who expresses the principles of love, compassion, forgiveness and acceptance.

CONSCIOUSNESS PRESENT MOMENT
This moment, right now. This is the only real moment, compared to past and future moments which are concepts in the mind.

CONSCIOUSNESS, MASS
The total vibration or feeling of all human consciousness. In each moment, all humans create a mass consciousness or vibrational resonance.

CONSCIOUSNESS, GROUP
The total feeling of a group of people. The humans within the group create a spiritual dimension. Groups include family, social groups, public spaces, work settings or internet gatherings.

CONSCIOUSNESS, UNITY
The feeling of oneness with all beings everywhere and Divine Source.

COUNCIL, SOUL'S JOURNEY
The Soul's Journey Council is 1000 to 2000 or more Masters interacting with the soul at some point along the 1200 lifetimes of experience. Each Master participates in the deliberation process about the soul's maturity to graduate from physicality.

COUNCIL, LIFETIME
The Lifetime Council is 20-50 Masters that guide the soul during the experience. This council deliberates on the karmic scoreboard at the conclusion of the life. This council governs karmic events, rewards, blessings and hears prayer requests.

COUNCIL, PRIMARY
The Primary Council is 10-12 Masters guiding all of the soul's journey. These Masters are closest to the soul.

COSMIC DIMENSIONS
A scale from 1 to 10 that exemplifies spiritual progress in humans.

COSMIC RAY

An energy from Divine Source affecting human spiritual evolution. When the Cosmic Ray is projecting strongly, humans move up in dimensional consciousness.

DESTINY

The potential outcome of a human story. Destiny is not written in stone but occurs when one stays on course and follows its path.

DIVINATION TOOLS

A tool allowing communication with Light Beings. A practitioner attuned to Light will invite communication from the Light Realms. Tools include: angel cards, pendulum, crystals, runes, I-Ching, tea leaf reading, dowsing rod, sacred geometry, sacred space and other methods.

DIVINE LINE

A component of the Energy Body that holds the 100 chakras and connects to Divine Source. Also known as the white cord in other spiritual text.

DIVINE SOURCE

An energy that created all, an ocean of bliss, a field of white light, consciousness. The energy of Divine Source is love, peace and joy. Divine Source is known as God, Prime Creator, Divine Mother and Heavenly Father.

DREAMTIME

During sleep, the Lightbody or Lightbody travels to the Light Realms.

EMPATHY

A spiritual gift where one can feel the emotions and energies of people and places.

ENERGY BODY

The energy body is also known as the astral body, etheric body, vital body or angelic body. It is energy based and not seen with physical eyes.

ENERGY, PRANIC

A flow of energy that comes from Divine Source that contains love. It is known by several names in energy practices. It is called prana, chi, ki, energy, life force, or white light energy. In the Christian church, it is known as Holy Spirit.

ENERGY HEALER

A person who utilizes energy from Divine Source to clear blocks in the energy body. Blocks are traumatic emotions and negative energies.

FATE

A predestined meeting with another soul. This arrangement is necessary to provide some aspect that helps one develop their story.

FIVE ASPECTS OF THE SELF

Five components of the human with different functions that work together as a whole unit. It consists of the physical body, the mental body, the emotional body, the energetic body and the soulful body, also known as the Lightbody.

FREE WILL AND CHOICE

A condition of our solar system ordered by Divine Source. It allows humans to be disconnected from Divine Source and make their own decisions about spirituality and integrity in the light.

FRUITS OF THE SPIRITS

Qualities of the spiritual student that develop during their journey.

The fruits are love, joy, peace, patience, kindness, goodness, gentleness, faithfulness and self-control. This list is referenced in the Christian Bible.

FULL DISCLOSURE

The concept that world governments are withholding information about intelligent life. The hope that governments will fully disclose what is known.

GAIA

Gaia is the spiritual name of Earth, and also representing the soul's essence of Earth.

GALACTICS

An entity with a physical form originating in other regions of the Astrodome, or universe. They are known as aliens or unidentified beings.

GALACTICS, HUMAN

Humans are galactics that reside on Earth.

HIGHERSELF

An aspect of the Lightbody, or Lightbody, residing in Divine Source.

JESUS CHRIST

The human embodiment of Christ Consciousness. The physical form of God as referenced in the Christian religion. Considered Son of God by Divine Source and appointed highest ranking Master in the Light Realms and Earth.

KARMA

Karma is recorded history of wrong choices where one harmed themselves or another person.

KARMA, DELIBERATION OF

At the end of a lifetime, the Lifetime Council of Masters deliberates and decides the new karmic score. The karmic score goes up or down depending on the outcome of the life story.

KARMA, IMMEDIATE

If one harms themselves or another, this energy returns to them. Immediate karma concludes its energy cycle in a short period of time or within that lifetime.

KARMA, RESOLVING

Souls have made mistakes, known and unknown. One needs to resolve karma through asking forgiveness and performing spiritual practice.

KARMA, TOTAL

Accumulated karma over lifetimes of experience. This is the soul's karmic tally, needing correction for wrong actions. The purpose of karma is to learn about love. This is also called karmic debt.

KARMA, ZERO POINT

The goal of the Karmic Game is to end with zero karmic points. There are no actions owed or needing to be experienced, the soul is granted ascension to the Light Realms.

KARMIC DEBT

Same definition as Total Karma.

KARMIC GAME

A law stating if a human harms themselves or another, they need to learn from their wrong action by living life in the other person's experience. This is also called the Wheel of Karma in spiritual text.

KARMIC KNOT

A karmic knot is defined as a relationship experience one is required to move through. One would prefer to walk away from the situation, but a karmic knot forces both to deal with the relationship.

KARMIC SCOREBOARD

A record of all wrong actions made during a soul's journey. The goal of the karmic game is to reduce the score to zero point, or hold no karmic debt.

LIFE LESSONS

A life lesson is a spiritual lesson a soul is attempting to master. It is considered a part of a spiritual curriculum. Examples of life lessons are unconditional love, patience, compassion and self-love.

LIFE PURPOSE

A predestined potential fulfilled during one's lifetime. The life purpose is a general concept, for example, to lead, teach, heal, be artistic, write or counsel to name a few. A soul can have more than one life purpose.

LIGHTBODY

An aspect of a human containing one's soul essence. The Higherself is an aspect of the Lightbody that resides in Divine Source. The Lightbody is also called the Lightbody in Five Aspects of the Self.

LIGHT BEINGS

An entity that resides in the Light Realms. A Light Being explores recreational realms in-between lives or after Ascension. Another category of Light Being is an angel or Masters, which have different types, roles and responsibilities.

LIGHT REALMS

A realm without darkness, also known as Heaven in the Christian Bible.

LIGHTWORKERS

A human 5th dimensional or higher. They fulfill a purpose to bring light to a dark world. They incarnated to be healers and helpers.

MASTERS, EARTH

A Light Being incarnated on Earth serving as a model for how to live one's life. There is history and spiritual text about their mission.

MASTERS, WHITE LIGHT

A Light Being appointed to guide humans and direct the course of their life. These Masters are not referenced in spiritual text.

MEDITATION

A spiritual practice where one rests the physical body, stills the mind, attunes emotions to love, clears the energy body and fills with Divine Source.

MORAL CODE

An understanding of right and wrong actions. When a soul is conscious of karma one has a strong moral code. There is no harm done to one or another.

MULTI-DIMENSIONALITY

The awareness that one travels to different dimensions beyond the physical realm.

PAST LIVES

The conscious knowingness one has lived prior lifetimes on Earth or on other planets.

PRANA

A particle of energy that comes from Divine Source that contains love. It is called prana in yogic text. It is known by several names in energy practices. It is called chi, ki, energy, life force, or white light energy. In the Christian church it is known as Holy Spirit.

PSYCHIC SKILLS

Gifts given by Divine Source to assist one in healing themselves and others. Psychic refers to gifts from the unseen or energy realms. These gifts are also known as spiritual gifts and open when one advances in spiritual consciousness.

PURIFICATION

The act of purifying oneself through spiritual practice.

PERCEIVED REALITIES

A psychic skill or spiritual gift where one perceives realities beyond the physical dimension.

RECOGNITION OF HUMANITY

The meaning of the word Namaste is realized. The light within honors and recognizes the light within all. Regardless of our cosmic dimension, all are aspects of Divine Source.

SPIRITUAL AWARENESS

The understanding one is a spiritual being. One creates their own unique path aligned to Divine Source. An understanding that all religions have a singular message: love yourself, love others, love the Earth and love Divine Source.

SPIRITUAL BYPASSING

The act of developing psychic skills and channeling without being aligned to Divine Source. This can invite negative or dark entities that guide the soul down an incorrect path.

Spiritual Gifts Gifts given by Divine Source, assisting in healing oneself and others. Spiritual gifts are known as psychic skills.

SPIRITUAL HYPNOSIS

A hypnosis session with the intention of experiencing a past-life regression, the astral realms or one's Higherself.

SPIRITUAL PRACTICE

Any exercise or spiritual ritual performed frequently devoted to Divine Source. Spiritual growth, purification and resolving karmic debt are benefits of spiritual practice.

SPIRITUALITY

The awareness a soul is spiritual, meaning non-physical. A comprehension that spirit is eternal and a part of Divine Source.

THE SOUL'S CONTRACT

See the reference for 'the Soul's Journey'.

THE SOUL'S JOURNEY

When a soul incarnates, it commits to live approximately 1200 lifetimes of experience. Each set of 1200 lifetimes is a soul's journey. The soul is working towards purification, mastering light lessons, having zero karma, feeling beautiful and free from worldly attachments. Also known as 'the soul's contract'.

TELEPATHY

A spiritual gift or psychic skill in which one connects with another through thoughts.

TRANCE STATES

Also known as altered states of consciousness. In a trance state, one moves their consciousness to a higher dimension. Meditation and hypnosis are examples of trance states.

VOLUNTEERS

Souls who have incarnated from higher dimensions with the specific purpose to become Lightworkers. Volunteers intuitively want to be healers and helpers. They have spiritual gifts and psychic skills to assist them in their missions.

NOTES

NOTES

NOTES

NOTES

Printed in the United States
By Bookmasters